United States History

Robert Taggart

JWW382 v1.02

POWER BASICS®

Senior Author .... Robert Taggart
Editorial Director .... Susan Blair
Project Manager .... Maggie Jones
Project Editor .... Erica Varney
Director of Marketing .... Jeff Taplin
Senior Production Editor .... Maggie Jones
Interior Design .... Mark Sayer
Cover Design .... Roman Laszok
Typesetting .... Sheila Russell
Mark Sayer
Ian Weidner
Editorial Staff .... Elizabeth Lynch
Richard Lynch
Holly Moirs
Kate O'Halloran
Mary Rich

ISBN 978-0-8251-5661-8

J. Weston Walch, Publisher
10200 Jefferson Blvd. | Culver City, CA 90232
www.socialstudies.com/walch
Printed in the United States of America

Table of Contents

To the Student

Welcome to the *Power Basics ® United States History.* This book will teach you all about the founding and development of our nation. You will learn about the history of the United States from the first colonies to the first part of the twenty-first century.

Unit 1: Birth of a Nation presents the early years of United States history, from colonization to the early years of independence. You will learn about the factors that brought Europeans to the New World, the original confederation of states, the U.S. Constitution, and the impacts of the nation's leaders in the early years of independence.

Unit 2: Development of the Nation I tells about the development of the United States from the early 1800s through the years after the Civil War. You will examine the causes of the nation's westward expansion and the causes and results of the Civil War, including the postwar Reconstruction era.

Unit 3: Development of the Nation II presents the development of the United States during the late 1800s and the early 1900s. You will learn about the nation's industrialization and urbanization in the late 1800s, issues related to immigration, and the shifts between isolationism and internationalism in U.S. history.

Unit 4: Twentieth-Century America and Beyond covers the development of the United States during the 1900s and early 2000s. You will explore the events, people, and trends of U.S. history during the Great Depression, World War II, the Cold War, and the years after the events of 9/11.

Power Basics United States History has many special features that make learning easier. Tip sections give you hints on ways to master the ideas and facts in the text. "In Real Life" sections give you examples of real-life events and people that will help you relate to the information you are learning. "Think About It" questions ask you to look at facts in a new way. The text also features "portrait" sections, which give you

To the Student, *continued*

mini-biographies of important historical figures. And the "Words to Know" section at the start of each lesson includes important new terms introduced in the book. The words appear in the Glossary at the end of the book. Finally, the Appendixes at the back of the book include further useful information.

As you move through *Power Basics United States History,* you will become more informed about your country, its innovative government, and its varied and dynamic people. We hope that you enjoy this material as you learn.

UNIT 1

Birth of a Nation

LESSON 1: From Colonization to Independence

GOAL: To understand the factors that brought Europeans to the New World and caused them to seek independence

WORDS TO KNOW

Boston Massacre

Boston Tea Party

colonies

colonists

commander in chief

debt

Declaration of Independence

foreign policy

Indian Wars

Indians

Loyalists

Native Americans

New World

Parliament

reconcile

Redcoats

religious freedom

revolution

trade

treaty

Treaty of Paris

The First Americans

The first European explorers came to North America while looking for a shorter route to India. When they arrived, they found that there were already many people living here. These people were **Native Americans**. They had been living on the land for a long time. There were hundreds of Native American nations. Each nation had its own name, culture, and language.

The European explorers did not call these people Native Americans. They knew that the people of India were darker-skinned than most Europeans. When they saw the darker-skinned Native Americans, they thought they had arrived in India. So, they called them **Indians**.

After the explorers, other Europeans came. They were mainly from three countries: England, France, and Spain. By then, everyone knew that they had not reached India. They called this new place the **New World.** The people who came to settle in the New World were called **colonists.** Colonists are people who make their homes in a new land but remain citizens of their native country.

The new settlers often threatened the Native Americans' way of life. Sometimes relations between the groups were peaceful. But as more settlers came, there were more conflicts (fights). The Native American nations fought for what they thought were their lands. But, the settlers believed that the lands were now theirs. These conflicts were called the **Indian Wars.** They lasted, off and on, for hundreds of years.

There were about one million Native Americans in North America when the Europeans first arrived. By the time the wars ended, there were only about 200,000. But, the wars did not cause most of these deaths. Native Americans had no immunity to European diseases. (Immunity is the power to resist a disease.) The native people of the Americas were killed in huge numbers by diseases such as measles, chicken pox, smallpox, and influenza (flu).

The people who made the difficult voyage to the New World had many reasons for doing so. Some came for the adventure of settling a new land. Many expected to find riches here. Other settlers came to find a better life for themselves and their families. In Europe, farmers had to pay high rents and taxes. In the New World, there seemed to be endless land for farming. The settlers considered this land to be free. They did not pay the Native Americans for the land. This "free" land attracted more and more people to the New World. With high hopes, they came to settle the land and develop farming communities.

Another important reason for coming to the New World was religion. In Europe, some people had been treated cruelly because of their religious beliefs. They came to the New World looking for **religious freedom.** For example, the Puritans, a Protestant group, left England and settled in Massachusetts. Also, an Englishman named Lord Baltimore founded the colony of Maryland as a place of religious freedom for Catholics.

THINK ABOUT IT

Many people feel that the European settlers robbed the Native Americans of their land. The Native Americans had already been living in the region for many years before the Europeans "discovered" it. But, as soon as the European explorers found the land, they considered it to be their own. Do you think this was fair? How would you have felt if you were a Native American who was suddenly forced to live under foreign rule? Write your answer on a separate sheet of paper.

PRACTICE 1: The First Americans

Decide if each statement below is true (**T**) or false (**F**). Write the correct letter on the line before each statement.

_____ **1.** The first European explorers came to North America while looking for a route to India.

_____ **2.** The Native Americans fought to keep their lands.

_____ **3.** Colonists are people who move to a new land but remain citizens of their native land.

England's Control

England was mostly interested in setting up colonies along the East Coast of North America—the land closest to the Atlantic Ocean. In time, there were 13 colonies along the East Coast. **Colonies** are regions controlled by distant countries. The 13 colonies were

Connecticut	New Hampshire	Rhode Island
Delaware	New Jersey	South Carolina
Georgia	New York	Virginia
Maryland	North Carolina	
Massachusetts	Pennsylvania	

13 Colonies

The people in the 13 colonies had come from England, Germany, Switzerland, and other European countries. However, by 1765, they were all under English control. King George III was the ruler. He and the English **Parliament**, or legislature, kept tight control over the colonies. They wanted to stay in charge of the colonies' dealings with other countries. The English declared that they would control the colonies' **foreign policy** and **trade**. This meant that England would be in charge of all business between the colonies and other countries.

The English Parliament also began to tax the colonists. This meant that the colonists had to pay England certain fees to live on and use the land.

England's strict control of foreign trade and policy began to anger the colonists more and more. The population of the New World was increasing. There was more farming and more trading. As they gained resources, the colonists wanted to trade directly with foreign countries. The colonists also wanted more rights. They were tired of being treated like second-class citizens. Also, the colonists did not think it was fair that they had to pay taxes to England since they could not vote for its government. Besides, England was far away. How could it rule them fairly?

There was no one in England to represent (speak for) the colonists. But, some colonists began to speak up for themselves. They declared, "No taxation without representation." This meant that the colonists refused to pay taxes if they could not elect anyone to represent them in England.

Sometimes the colonists did more than just speak out. There were acts of violence as colonists expressed their opposition to England's rule. Finally, war broke out. It was a **revolution**, a fight to overthrow a government. To stand up to England, the colonies formed an army. George Washington was appointed **commander in chief**, or head, of the army.

PRACTICE 2: England's Control

Circle the letter of the correct answer to each of the following questions.

1. Who tried to control the colonies' foreign policy and trade?
- **a.** Native Americans
- **b.** the English Parliament
- **c.** a small group of wealthy colonists
- **d.** the explorers

2. What is a revolution?
- **a.** a peaceful agreement
- **b.** a world war
- **c.** a fight to overthrow a government
- **d.** a nonviolent protest

The American Revolution

The war between the colonists and England began in 1775. The war started because the colonists wanted the English Parliament to give them more rights. In 1776, the colonists decided that they were through taking orders from England. They claimed to be a free nation, separate from England. The colonists did this in a document that they called the **Declaration of Independence.**

However, the colonists' statement of independence was not enough. Colonial troops had to continue fighting long and hard against England. At times, things looked hopeless for the new nation. Countries such as France, Spain, and the Netherlands gave the colonial army money and weapons to help their cause. Still, it looked as though England would win.

But, the colonists did not give up. They continued to fight, and the revolution took a turn. Finally, colonial troops defeated British troops in 1783. Soon after, the United States was recognized as a new nation.

Below are some of the major events that took place before and during the war.

- In 1768, 4,000 English soldiers took over the city of Boston, Massachusetts. The English knew that Boston was a place where many colonists had spoken out against English rule. Many colonists were forced to surrender their homes to English soldiers without payment.
- One day in 1770, a group of boys threw snowballs at some English soldiers. The soldiers were standing in a square outside the Boston State House. A fight followed, and a number of people became involved. The soldiers shot at the growing crowd, killing five people. This event was called the **Boston Massacre**.

The Boston Massacre, 1770

- In 1773, England tried to force the colonists to import tea from only one English company. They refused to do it. Instead, a group of colonists disguised themselves as Native Americans. They boarded the tea ships in Boston Harbor and threw the tea overboard. This is called the **Boston Tea Party** of 1773. The English were enraged. They closed down the city of Boston completely. The colonists realized they would soon have to fight for their rights.

- The British actions caused the colonies to unite in defense of Massachusetts. Colonists met in Philadelphia in 1774 at the first Continental Congress. They discussed ways to resist England.

- The first real shots of the war were fired on April 19, 1775, in Lexington, Massachusetts. Three months later, George Washington was appointed to his post as commander in chief of the colonial army.

- On July 4, 1776, the colonies declared their freedom in the Declaration of Independence. They no longer wanted to be a part of England.

- England refused to recognize the Declaration of Independence. It would not grant the colonies their independence. So, the war continued. In battle after battle, more soldiers were killed.

- The Declaration of Independence did help the colonists get financial support from other countries. France joined forces with the colonies in 1778, Spain in 1779, and the Netherlands in 1780. These countries provided extra money and supplies that the colonists needed to win the war. Some of these countries also sent soldiers to help the colonists fight the English. One Frenchman, the Marquis de Lafayette, was a great aid to the Americans. He helped Washington defeat the English at Yorktown, Virginia, in 1781.

- By 1783, the war was over. Colonial troops had triumphed. A peace treaty between England and the United States was signed in Paris, France. A **treaty** is an agreement or a contract between countries. Some treaties end wars. In the **Treaty of Paris**, England recognized the American colonies as a free and independent nation. The two countries agreed that America's boundaries were the Great Lakes in the north and the Mississippi River in the west.

REVOLUTIONARY PORTRAIT

Crispus Attucks (1723–1770)

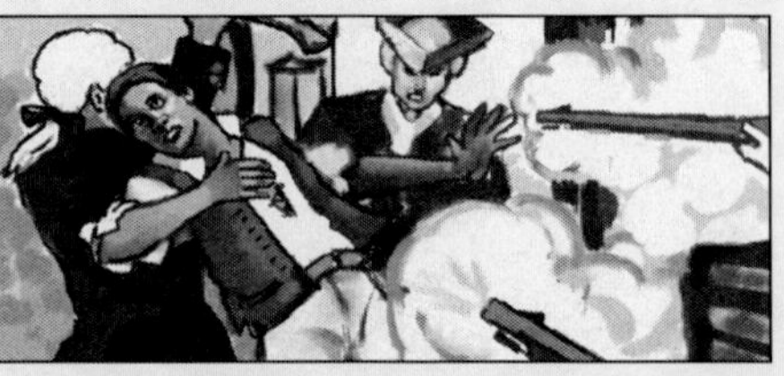

Crispus Attucks may have been the first man killed in the American Revolution. Attucks, a man of mixed African and Native American descent, had been a slave. But, he escaped slavery and became a seaman. Attucks was shot by English soldiers during the Boston Massacre. A statue of Attucks now stands on Boston Common, a few short blocks from where he, and four others, died.

PRACTICE 3: The American Revolution

Circle the letter of the correct answer to each of the following questions.

1. What started the Boston Massacre?

- **a.** Colonists were forced to give up their homes to English soldiers.
- **b.** England forced the colonists to buy tea from a certain company.
- **c.** Several boys threw snowballs at English soldiers.
- **d.** The English Parliament declared war.

2. When did the colonies declare their independence?

- **a.** 1783
- **b.** 1775
- **c.** 1770
- **d.** 1776

3. Which of the following statements is TRUE?

- **a.** The war ended in 1776 when the colonies declared their independence.
- **b.** French soldiers helped colonial troops fight against England.
- **c.** The main purpose of the Declaration of Independence was to ask France for help.
- **d.** Crispus Attucks was an English soldier killed during the Boston Massacre.

IN REAL LIFE

The American Revolution was the result of the colonists' protest against English rule. That revolution did not end protests for all time. Today, instead of revolution, people have other ways of protesting things they do not like about the government. Here are some ways people can protest:

- They can **vote** against a person or an issue if they do not agree.
- They can **write a letter** of protest to their representative.
- They can **organize** other citizens who feel the same way they do.
- They can **sign petitions** to change something they do not like. (A petition is a paper that takes a position on an issue.)
- They can **give money** to support the causes or candidates they believe in.
- They can **demonstrate** in public to show that they do not agree.

The Declaration of Independence

In 1776, shortly after the war began, a group of men from all of the colonies met. They voted to free themselves from England's rule. Their arguments for independence were summed up in one document, or paper. It was called the Declaration of Independence. The Declaration outlined the colonists' complaints against England. It also gave their reasons for wanting independence. There are three important principles, or ideas, in this document. They are as follows:

- The colonies are free and independent of England.
- All men are equal.

- Governments are set up to protect the rights of the people, and they receive their powers from the people.

At first, some of the colonists opposed separation. They wanted to **reconcile** with England. That is, they thought the colonies could work out their problems with England. But, in the end, these people agreed to break with England. The Declaration of Independence was signed on July 4, 1776.

Public reading of the Declaration of Independence, 1776

PRACTICE 4: The Declaration of Independence

Circle the letter of the correct answer to each of the following questions.

1. Which of the following statements did NOT appear in the Declaration of Independence?

- **a.** The colonies are free and independent.
- **b.** All slaves must be freed.
- **c.** All men are equal.
- **d.** Governments are set up to protect the rights of the people.

2. When was the Declaration of Independence signed?

- **a.** July 14, 1789
- **b.** January 1, 1776
- **c.** July 4, 1776
- **d.** May 29, 1779

THINK ABOUT IT

Many of the colonists wanted independence from England. But, others wanted to keep their ties to England. These people were called **Loyalists**, because they wanted to stay *loyal* to England. Loyalists did not support the revolution. Put yourself in the place of a person who has just arrived in the New World. Can you think of any reasons for *not* wanting to rebel against England? Write your answer on a separate sheet of paper.

The Colonists Win the War

How did the colonists win a war against a great power like England? There were several reasons. Some are listed below.

- In many ways, the colonists had better strategies for fighting. The way armies fought in those days was to meet another army on a battlefield. Row after row of soldiers would shoot at other rows of soldiers. But, the colonists fought more like the Native Americans. They would dart in and out of the trees, firing when they saw a target. The English soldiers made good targets because they wore brightly colored uniforms. These uniforms earned them the name **Redcoats.**

- The French and Spanish helped the colonists fight against England. These countries had many reasons for entering the war. One reason was to get back at England for past wars.

- Many of the English generals did not take the war seriously. They thought that they would win without a problem. As a result, they were careless and made many mistakes.

Once the war was over and the treaty was signed, the new nation still had many problems to solve. One major problem was that the long war had put the country in **debt.** This meant that they owed money to other people. Also, the 13 colonies, now called states, had to learn to work together. It was not going to be easy.

The English Surrender at Yorktown

IN REAL LIFE

Sometimes songs come to stand for certain events in our lives. When the English surrendered at Yorktown, the story goes that an English band played a song called "The World Turned Upside Down." This song became a theme song for the end of the revolution. Many people on both sides were shocked by the colonists' success. They probably felt as though the world was turning upside down when the British lost.

PRACTICE 5: The Colonists Win the War

Decide if each statement below is true (**T**) or false (**F**). Write the correct letter on the line before each statement.

_____ **1.** The Americans learned their fighting strategies from the Native Americans.

_____ **2.** English soldiers were called Redcoats because they wore brightly colored uniforms.

_____ **3.** France and Spain refused to help the colonists during the war.

_____ **4.** Many English generals did not want to go to war with the colonies because they were afraid they would lose.

_____ **5.** At the end of the war, the United States was a wealthy and an organized nation.

_____ **6.** The United States owed a lot of money after the war ended.

TIP

A time line can help you organize events that take place over a period of time. The time line below shows some events that took place during the period leading to American independence. Note that the earliest date, 1768, appears on the far left. The later years appear to the right. The last year, 1783, is the farthest right. Above the time line, a few words describe what happened on each of the dates on the time line.

English troops occupy Boston	Boston Massacre	Boston Tea Party	First shots fired	Colonies declare independence	The American Revolution ends
1768	1770	1773	1775	1776	1783

LESSON 2: Confederation

GOAL: To understand the reasons for the original confederation of states and to examine its strengths and weaknesses

WORDS TO KNOW

abolish
accomplishments
Articles of Confederation
authority
commerce
confederation
congress
Congress
Constitution
Constitutional Convention
delegates
federal
governor
issue currency
ratified
representatives
revise
Second Continental Congress
security
stable

A National Government

In 1775, there were 13 English colonies along the eastern coast of North America. Each colony had a separate government. A **governor** ran the affairs of each colony. However, the colonists had to work together as a group to stand up against England. In an attempt to unite, each colony chose **representatives**, or people who could speak for the others. These representatives became members of the **Second Continental Congress**. This group met in Philadelphia in 1775. Their job was to create a central, or national, government.

The Second Continental Congress did several things. It set up an army to fight against England. It wrote the Declaration of Independence. It also wrote a set of guidelines, or rules, for the new government. These rules were called the **Articles of Confederation**. A **confederation** is a group of states or nations that band together but still remain independent. The

Articles went into effect only after all 13 colonies **ratified**, or voted to accept, them. They did not get final approval until 1781.

The time line below shows the major events that led to the birth of the United States.

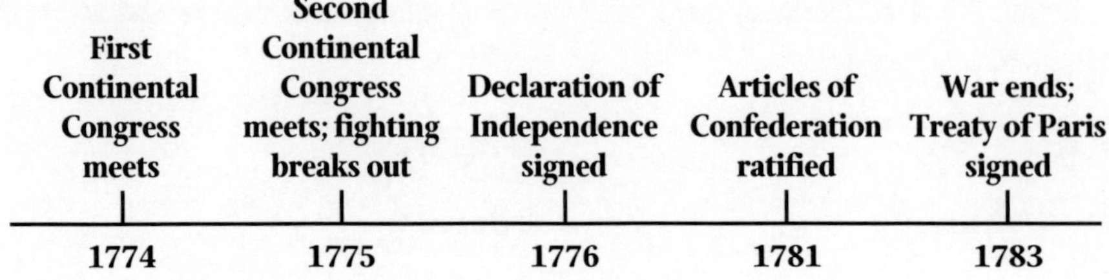

PRACTICE 6: A National Government

Circle the letter of the correct answer to each of the following questions.

1. What were the guidelines for the new country called?
  a. the Declaration of Independence
  b. the Articles of Confederation
  c. the Treaty of Paris
  d. the Second Continental Congress

2. Who set up the guidelines for the national government?
  a. the king of England
  b. the First Continental Congress
  c. the president of the United States
  d. the Second Continental Congress

The Powers of Congress

Under the Articles of Confederation, the central government was run by a national congress. A **congress** is a group of people who represent, or stand for, other people. The Articles gave **Congress** certain powers. However, it was very careful not to give Congress too much **authority**, or power. After winning their independence from England, the colonies did not want to give too much power to any one person or group.

The Articles of Confederation said that Congress could handle relations with other nations. It could also make treaties with those nations. If a peaceful agreement were not possible, Congress could declare war.

Congress also had the power to make laws and **issue currency**. This means that it had the right to make paper money and coins. In addition, Congress could try to settle disputes between the states.

The Articles of Confederation also listed some powers that Congress would *not* have. For example, Congress could not control **commerce** (the buying or selling of goods) among the states. While the colonies were under English rule, King George III and the English Parliament kept tight control over commerce. This is why the states did not want to hand this power over to Congress.

Also, Congress did not have the authority to collect taxes. The colonies had had to pay many different kinds of taxes to the English government. After they declared their independence, they did not want to have to pay such taxes again.

Look at the chart below. It shows what Congress could and could not do under the Articles of Confederation.

Congress Could . . .	Congress Could Not . . .
■ make agreements with other nations ■ declare war ■ make laws ■ print money ■ settle disagreements between states	■ control trade between the states ■ collect taxes

■ PRACTICE 7: The Powers of Congress

Circle the letter of the correct answer(s) to each of the following questions.

1. Which of the following powers did Congress NOT have under the Articles of Confederation? (*Hint:* There is more than one correct answer.)
   - **a.** the power to make laws
   - **b.** the power to collect taxes
   - **c.** the power to print money
   - **d.** the power to control trade between states

2. Why did the colonists decide NOT to give Congress the power to control commerce?
   a. because the English had controlled it so tightly
   b. because it would raise prices
   c. because the members of Congress argued so much
   d. because Congress had done this so badly before

TIP

When you look at the chart on page 17, you can quickly see what Congress could and could not do. A chart like this one makes information easy to read and remember. You can also use a chart to help you study for an exam. Just make a blank chart in your notebook. Give it headings that make sense. Then, copy information from your notes into the chart as you study. Writing the information into the chart will help you remember it. You can also study the chart a day or two before the exam for a quick review.

A Weak Central Government

The Articles of Confederation were the first step toward a unified nation. Yet, they did not create a strong, **stable** government (one that could be depended on). The first government of the United States had too many weaknesses. Here are four main reasons why the government was weak.

- The Articles did not provide for a real head of government, such as a president.
- They did not provide for a system of courts and judges. Each state set up its own courts and appointed its own judges.
- They gave more power to the states than to the **federal** (national) government.
- The federal government could not enforce laws passed by Congress.

After years of rule by England, the states did not want to give too much power to a central government. They liked the **security**, or safety, of having other states on their side in a loose confederation. Yet, they also liked their independence. Each state therefore made its own laws. Each had its own tax system. Each had its own courts. The problem was that this group of independent states did not work well as a country.

IN REAL LIFE

Today, the currency you use is made up of dollars and cents. Coins and paper money were first introduced into North America by various European settlers. England did not issue money for the colonists, though. Instead, the colonists used tobacco, shell beads, and Spanish "pieces of eight," coins known as *dollars.* The colonists also issued their own paper money, called *bills.* When the colonists broke with England, they paid for the American Revolution with paper dollars issued by the Continental Congress in 1775.

PRACTICE 8: A Weak Central Government

Decide if each statement below is true (**T**) or false (**F**). Write the correct letter on the line before each statement.

_____ **1.** The Articles of Confederation did not establish a strong, stable government.

_____ **2.** The Articles of Confederation named the first U.S. president.

_____ **3.** The Articles of Confederation gave more power to the federal government than to the states.

_____ **4.** The federal government could not make laws, but they could enforce them.

_____ **5.** Under the Articles of Confederation, each state set up its own courts and chose its own judges.

The Constitutional Convention

In 1787, a group of men from 12 states met in Philadelphia, Pennsylvania, to **revise** (change) the Articles of Confederation. (Rhode Island was the only state that refused to send a representative.) Many of the men who came to this meeting thought that they could strengthen the government by revising the Articles. Others felt that the country needed a new set of guidelines. They convinced the group to start from scratch. Instead of revising the Articles of Confederation, they wrote a completely new document. They wrote the **Constitution** of the United States. More than 200 years later, this document still serves as the highest law in the United States.

State House in Philadelphia

The gathering in Philadelphia became known as the **Constitutional Convention**. The **delegates** (people chosen to attend the convention) were important state officials. There were governors, judges, and officers of the law. There were also lawyers, doctors, soldiers, clergymen, merchants, and farmers. Many had been involved in the Revolutionary War. Among the delegates were future presidents George Washington and James Madison. Washington was president of the convention. Madison probably did more than any other man to shape the Constitution. Two other famous delegates were Benjamin Franklin and Alexander Hamilton.

CONSTITUTIONAL PORTRAIT

Benjamin Franklin (1706–1790)

Benjamin Franklin did so many things well that it is hard to say what his greatest **accomplishments**, or successes, were. He was a writer, scientist, inventor, politician, diplomat, and thinker. One of the things he did best was to inspire others to get things done. For example, Franklin helped establish libraries, schools, and organizations to encourage advanced thinking. He also worked with Thomas Jefferson on the Declaration of Independence. At the Constitutional Convention, Franklin played a key role in creating the final document. His last political act was to sign a request that Congress **abolish**, or end, slavery.

PRACTICE 9: The Constitutional Convention

Circle the letter of the correct answer to each of the following questions.

1. Why did state delegates attend the Constitutional Convention of 1787?

- **a.** to write new guidelines for the U.S. government
- **b.** to revise the Constitution
- **c.** to revise the Articles of Confederation
- **d.** to write a document that asked Congress to end slavery

2. What happened at the Constitutional Convention?

- **a.** the delegates wrote a brand-new set of guidelines for the U.S. government
- **b.** the delegates revised the Articles of Confederation
- **c.** the delegates voted for the first president and vice president of the United States
- **d.** none of the above

3. What was Benjamin Franklin's last political act?

- **a.** He signed the Declaration of Independence.
- **b.** He helped write the Constitution.
- **c.** He was elected president.
- **d.** He signed a request asking Congress to abolish slavery.

THINK ABOUT IT

Even today, people disagree about how much power Congress should have. In fact, you can hear this discussed during most presidential elections. Some people think that the states should have more power. Others believe that it is important to have a strong central government. Listen to the arguments. Both sides will be expressing some of the same concerns that the delegates at the Constitutional Convention had. What do you think? Should the federal government have more or less power than it has now? Write your answer on a separate sheet of paper.

LESSON 3: Framing the Constitution

GOAL: To identify the most important parts of the U.S. Constitution and to understand the historical reasons for their being included

WORDS TO KNOW

amendments

bicameral

Bill of Rights

checks and balances

compromise

concurrent powers

democracy

Elastic Clause

executive branch

expressed powers

federalism

guarantee

House of Representatives

implied powers

judicial branch

legislative branch

legislature

Necessary and Proper Clause

originate

philosophy

prohibited

reserved powers

self-government

separation of powers

Senate

senators

taxation

Three-Fifths Compromise

The Constitution

As you have learned, the Constitutional Convention was called to revise the Articles of Confederation. Instead, the delegates wrote a new document called the Constitution of the United States of America.

The delegates at the Constitutional Convention had a difficult job. They had to find a way to give the federal government more power than it had under the Articles of Confederation. At the same time, they did not want to take too much power from the states. In this lesson, you will learn how the writers of the Constitution dealt with this issue and many others.

The Constitution explains the rules for running the government of the United States. The most important principle in the Constitution is **self-government**. This means that the U.S. government is ruled by the people. Another name for this type of government is a **democracy**.

According to the Constitution, the people of the United States can control the government by electing representatives. Representatives are people you vote for to make decisions for you. Representatives speak up for the people. Through their representatives, the people can make and change laws.

The Constitution has remained the highest law of the United States. Every person and every organization in the United States must follow its rules. There are no exceptions, including the government itself.

■ PRACTICE 10: The Constitution

Decide if each statement below is true (**T**) or false (**F**). Write the correct letter on the line before each statement.

_____ **1.** The president of the United States does not have to follow the rules of the Constitution.

_____ **2.** The Constitution still serves as the nation's highest law.

_____ **3.** According to the Constitution, the U.S. government is run by the American people.

Federalism

The first and most important thing the delegates at the Constitutional Convention had to decide was how to balance power between the federal government and the states. To solve this issue, the delegates decided the basic **philosophy**, or way of thinking, of the Constitution. It is called **federalism**.

Under federalism, power is divided between the federal government and the state governments. Certain powers belong to each. The delegates divided the powers under four headings: expressed powers, implied powers, reserved powers, and concurrent powers.

Expressed powers are the powers of the federal government. These powers are expressed, or stated directly, in the Constitution. Some examples of expressed powers are the power to coin money and the power to raise an army and a navy.

Implied powers are also powers of the federal government. But, these powers are not stated directly in the Constitution. They are implied, or suggested, in one of the expressed powers. These powers are granted to the federal government under a section of the document called the **Necessary and Proper Clause.** The purpose of this clause is to give the federal government the power to make laws that are necessary to carry out expressed powers. For example, the government has used implied powers to build interstate highway systems. It has also used implied powers to forbid discrimination in public places and to set up a national banking system.

TIP

The Necessary and Proper Clause is sometimes called the **Elastic Clause.** This is because it has often allowed the federal government to *stretch* its powers. For example, the Constitution states that the federal government has the power to tax and to raise money. However, it does not state exactly how the government is allowed to do this. Under the Elastic Clause, the federal government stretched its power to find a way. It set up a national banking system.

Reserved powers are the powers reserved, or kept, for the states. These powers are not listed in the Constitution. However, they include any powers that are not given to the federal government. For example, states have the power to control their own public health and education.

Concurrent powers are those that are shared by the federal government and the state governments. For example, both set taxes, borrow money, and build roads.

PRACTICE 11: Federalism

Circle the letter of the correct answer to each of the following questions.

1. What is federalism?
   - **a.** the division of power between federal and state governments
   - **b.** the name of the U.S. government under the Articles of Confederation
   - **c.** the powers given to state governments
   - **d.** the powers given to the federal government

2. Which of the following are powers given to state governments?
   - **a.** expressed powers
   - **b.** implied powers
   - **c.** reserved powers
   - **d.** both *a* and *b*

3. What is an example of a concurrent power?
   - **a.** the power to coin money
   - **b.** the power to raise an army
   - **c.** the power to set taxes
   - **d.** none of the above

Compromises of the Constitution

The delegates at the Constitutional Convention had to make decisions about many difficult issues. Different states wanted different things. There were many disagreements. For example, northern states disagreed with southern states. States that had large populations disagreed with states with small populations.

The delegates had to work hard to find ways to satisfy all the states. They did this by making compromises. A **compromise** is an agreement that tries to meet both sides of an issue. It usually requires both sides to give up a little of what they want. In return, each side also receives something it wants.

The Senate and the House of Representatives

One difficult issue was that of state representation in Congress. Congress is the **legislature**, or the lawmaking part of government. States with many people wanted representation to be based on population. However, this would give states with large populations more representatives. In turn, this would give those states more power. States with small populations did not like that plan. They wanted equal representation for each state.

To solve this problem, the delegates worked out a compromise. They agreed that the states would be represented in two ways. Congress would be **bicameral**. This meant that it would have two law-making houses—the Senate and the House of Representatives.

In the **Senate**, each state would have two representatives. The population of the state would not matter. The members of the Senate would be called **senators**.

In the **House of Representatives**, the number of representatives would be based on population. This meant that different states would have different numbers of representatives. States with larger populations would have more representatives than states with smaller populations. The members of the House of Representatives would be called representatives.

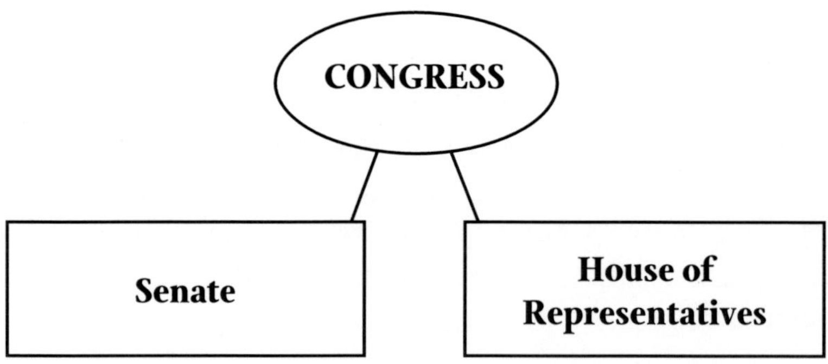

Taxation

The delegates also disagreed about taxation. **Taxation** is the way the government raises money by charging certain fees to citizens. According to the Constitution, people and businesses would not pay taxes directly to the federal government. Instead, they would pay taxes to the state. Only the states would pay taxes to the federal government. The delegates disagreed about how much each state would pay. States with small populations wanted taxes to be based on population. In this way, the more people there were in a state, the more taxes the state would pay to the federal government. States with large populations, though, wanted every state to pay the same amount of taxes.

Another part of the tax question was who in Congress would have the most say in raising and lowering taxes. States with small populations wanted tax bills to begin in the Senate. That way, they would have a vote that was equal to larger states. States with large populations wanted tax bills to begin in the House of Representatives, where they had more representation. That way, they would have more power.

The delegates finally decided on a compromise. It was agreed that tax bills would **originate**, or start, in the House of Representatives. However, states would be taxed according to population.

The Three-Fifths Compromise

A third difficult issue involved slaves. Congress debated whether slaves should be counted as part of the population. Since most slaves were in southern states, the southern states wanted slaves to be counted as part of the population. This way, their states would have more representatives in the House of Representatives. Northern states had a different point of view. Delegates from the northern states felt that since slaves could not vote or hold office, they should not be counted as part of the population.

The delegates finally settled on the **Three-Fifths Compromise**. Under this agreement, each slave would be counted as three fifths of a person.

PRACTICE 12: Compromises of the Constitution

Circle the letter of the correct answer to each of the following questions.

1. How many representatives from each state are there in the Senate?
- **a.** four
- **b.** two
- **c.** It depends on the size of the state.
- **d.** It depends on the population of the state.

2. How many representatives from each state are there in the House of Representatives?
   a. two
   b. ten
   c. It depends on the size of the state.
   d. It depends on the population of the state.

3. How did larger states want taxes to be paid?
   a. directly to the federal government by people and businesses
   b. equally by all the states
   c. mostly by smaller states
   d. based on population

4. What were the terms of the Three-Fifths Compromise?
   a. Small states would only pay three fifths of the taxes paid by larger states.
   b. The federal government would get three fifths of the taxes paid to it by the states.
   c. Only three fifths of all representatives had to approve a tax bill for it to pass.
   d. Each slave would be counted as only three fifths of a person.

The Three Branches of Government

The delegates at the Constitutional Convention decided to divide the government into three parts, or branches. They did this so that no one person or group of people would get too much power. By dividing the duties of the government, they divided its authority.

The Constitution describes the three branches of government. It also explains the duties and powers of each branch. The three branches are the **legislative branch**, the **executive branch**, and the **judicial branch**.

This division of power into three parts is called **separation of powers**. Together, the three branches share the power of the government. Each branch has its own governing duties. Look at the chart on page 29. It shows the name, main offices, and main duties of each branch.

Branch	Main Offices	Main Duties
Legislative	Congress (the House of Representatives and the Senate)	passes, or makes, the laws
Executive	the president and the vice president	enforces, or carries out, the laws
Judicial	the Supreme Court (the highest court in the country) and other courts	interprets, or explains, the laws

PRACTICE 13: The Three Branches of Government

Write the correct answer to each question on the line(s) provided.

1. What are the three branches of government?

_______________ _______________ _______________

2. What is the main duty of the judicial branch?

____

3. What is the main duty of the legislative branch?

____

4. What is the main duty of the executive branch?

____

Checks and Balances

The Constitution did more than just create three branches of government. It also established a system of **checks and balances**. This system provides ways for each of the three branches to check, or control, the other two. That way, no one branch can become too powerful or too weak.

The chart on page 30 explains how the system of checks and balances works. Each branch has the power to do one or more things to "check" the other two branches.

Checks and Balances

Executive

How can the executive branch check the judicial branch?	■ The president can pardon, or set free, people convicted in federal court.
How can the executive branch check the legislative branch?	■ The president can veto, or refuse to sign, acts that Congress has passed.

Legislative

How can the legislative branch check the executive branch?	■ Congress can override, or set aside, the president's veto. ■ Congress can impeach the president (accuse him or her of a federal crime).
How can the legislative branch check the judicial branch?	■ Congress must approve all federal judges.

Judicial

How can the judicial branch check the executive branch?	■ The Supreme Court can declare the president's acts to be against the Constitution.
How can the judicial branch check the legislative branch?	■ The Supreme Court can declare an act or a law of Congress to be against the Constitution.

The chart on page 30 gives just one example of a check for each category. The Constitution sets up a number of other checks. At different times in U.S. history, one branch or another has seemed to have the most power. But, the system of checks has continued to keep the power among the branches balanced.

IN REAL LIFE

The delegates at the Constitutional Convention did not want the country's president and vice president to be chosen by direct, or popular, vote. They felt that a popular election would lead to disagreement and disorder among the states. In those days, voters were scattered throughout the country. There were no television, radio, and national newspapers to inform them about the candidates. So, the delegates at the Convention chose *indirect* democracy instead. In indirect democracy, the presidential candidates are elected by representatives from each state.

Today, the president or vice president is not elected by direct vote. When citizens vote on Election Day, they are not actually voting for president. They are voting for representatives, who in turn vote for the president. Do you think this is still a good system?

PRACTICE 14: Checks and Balances

Circle the letter of the correct answer to each of the following questions.

1. What is the purpose of checks and balances?

- **a.** to give people the right to vote for president
- **b.** to regulate who is elected to Congress
- **c.** to balance power between the two houses of Congress
- **d.** to stop any one branch of government from getting too much power

2. How can the executive branch check the power of the legislative branch?
   a. by appointing federal judges
   b. by vetoing a bill
   c. by firing justices
   d. by overriding a veto

3. How can the judicial branch check the power of the executive branch?
   a. by declaring a president's acts to be against the Constitution
   b. by removing judges from the Supreme Court
   c. by vetoing a bill
   d. by overriding a veto

The Bill of Rights

Many delegates at the Constitutional Convention wanted the Constitution to protect people's rights. They wanted to give people a **guarantee**, or promise, that these rights would never change. The delegates decided to describe these rights in ten **amendments**, or changes, to the Constitution. These first ten amendments are known as the **Bill of Rights**. The Bill of Rights was ratified in 1791.

The Bill of Rights includes the following amendments:

- **First Amendment:** protects freedom of speech and religion
- **Second Amendment:** protects the right to own and carry guns
- **Third Amendment:** protects people from having to shelter soldiers in their homes against their wishes
- **Fourth Amendment:** protects people from "unreasonable searches" by the government
- **Fifth Amendment:** protects the right to "due process of law"; protects people from being tried for the same crime twice; protects

people from being forced to be witnesses against themselves; protects people from having their lives, freedom, or property taken without lawful action

- **Sixth Amendment:** protects a person's right to a fair trial
- **Seventh Amendment:** protects a person's right to have a trial by jury
- **Eighth Amendment:** protects people from cruel or unusual punishments if found guilty of a crime
- **Ninth Amendment:** protects individual rights not actually listed in the Constitution
- **Tenth Amendment:** protects states' rights

PRACTICE 15: The Bill of Rights

Circle the letter of the correct answer to each of the following questions.

1. What are the first ten amendments of the Constitution called?
   - **a.** the Rights of the People
   - **b.** the Bill of Rights
   - **c.** the Constitution Addition
   - **d.** the States' Rights

2. Which amendment protects people from having to shelter soldiers in their homes?
   - **a.** second
   - **b.** fourth
   - **c.** third
   - **d.** eighth

3. Which amendment protects other rights not listed in the Constitution?
   - **a.** sixth
   - **b.** seventh
   - **c.** eighth
   - **d.** ninth

4. Which amendment protects the rights of individual states?
   a. first
   b. fifth
   c. eighth
   d. tenth

Amending the Constitution

The Constitution was written in 1787. It is the oldest constitution in the world. Yet, the United States of today is very different from the United States of 1787. Why do you think the Constitution still works?

One very important reason is that the Constitution is open to change. The delegates at the convention realized that they needed to make the Constitution flexible. They knew that as time went on, the needs of people and society would change. So, they made rules within the Constitution that allowed for these changes.

Since the original Constitution was ratified in 1787, 17 further amendments have been added to it (other than the Bill of Rights). Some of these amendments are listed below. The year following each amendment is the year that it was ratified by the states.

- **Amendment 12 (1804):** changed the electoral college, which helps prevent ties in presidential elections
- **Amendment 13 (1865):** made slavery illegal
- **Amendment 14 (1868):** guaranteed all U.S. citizens equal protection under the law
- **Amendment 15 (1870):** gave all men the right to vote, regardless of race and color
- **Amendment 19 (1920):** gave women the right to vote
- **Amendment 22 (1951):** limited a U.S. president to serving no more than two terms
- **Amendment 24 (1964):** **prohibited** (outlawed) making anyone pay a tax to be allowed to vote
- **Amendment 26 (1971):** lowered the voting age to 18 years

TIP

You have just read short summaries of some amendments to the Constitution. You might also want to read about other amendments not mentioned here. Or, you may want to read the Constitution in its original language. You can find a copy of the Constitution in any edition of *The World Almanac.* You can also find it on the Internet at www.archives.gov/founding-docs/constitution

PRACTICE 16: Amending the Constitution

Circle the letter of the correct answer to each of the following questions.

1. Why did the writers of the Constitution make the document flexible?
   a. They did not have time to finish it.
   b. They could not agree on several issues.
   c. They knew it would not work.
   d. They knew that the needs of society would change over time.

2. How many amendments (not counting the Bill of Rights) have been ratified by the states since 1787?
   a. none
   b. 10
   c. 17
   d. 20

3. Which amendment gave women the right to vote?
   a. Amendment 26
   b. Amendment 19
   c. Amendment 15
   d. none of the above

4. When did slavery become illegal?
   a. 1787
   b. 1804
   c. 1865
   d. 1870

LESSON 4: The Founding Fathers

GOAL: To identify the founding fathers and to explain how their views blended to form a new kind of government

WORDS TO KNOW

agrarian

appointed

Cabinet

Democratic-Republican Party

Federalist Party

Founding Fathers

interpreted

political party

secretary of state

secretary of the treasury

tyranny

The First Presidents

The men who were part of the first federal government are often called the **Founding Fathers.** Most of these men helped to write the Constitution. They also took part in the Revolutionary War against England.

Some of the Founding Fathers also served as the country's first presidents. James Madison of Virginia, for example, became the nation's fourth president. Madison fought in the Revolutionary War and helped develop the Constitution. After the Constitutional Convention, Madison wrote and spoke wherever he could to persuade states to ratify the Constitution. That is why some people called him the Father of our Constitution.

James Madison

George Washington was another Founding Father and the first man to be elected president after the Constitution was ratified. He, too, had worked hard to see that the Constitution was written. As you have learned, Washington was commander in chief of the colonial army during the American Revolution. His leadership during the war won him the respect of his country. There was never any question that he would become the first president. Washington is sometimes called the Father of our Country.

PRESIDENTIAL PORTRAIT

George Washington (1732–1799)

First president of the United States
Vice president: John Adams
Term: 1789–1797
Party: Federalist
Home state: Virginia

Washington favored a strong central government. He took part in the writing of the Constitution and worked hard as president to follow its guidelines. During his presidency, he had to deal with other countries. Since his time, foreign policy has been the responsibility of the president.

PRACTICE 17: The First Presidents

Circle the letter of the correct answer to each of the following questions.

1. Which of the following statements does NOT describe James Madison?
- **a.** the nation's fourth president
- **b.** one of the nation's Founding Fathers
- **c.** fought for the British during the Revolution
- **d.** delegate at the Constitutional Convention

2. What is George Washington sometimes called?
- **a.** the Father of our Country
- **b.** the Father of our Constitution
- **c.** the Founder of the Constitution
- **d.** the Founder of our Nation

3. Which of the following statements about George Washington is NOT true?
- **a.** He was commander in chief of the colonial army.
- **b.** He was the first president of the United States.
- **c.** He favored a government with a weak central government and stronger state governments.
- **d.** He took part in the writing of the Constitution.

Washington and His Cabinet

Washington had a lot of work to do as the first president of the United States. However, he did not work alone. He had the help of his vice president, John Adams, and his **Cabinet**. The Cabinet was set up to advise the president. The first Cabinet had four executive departments.

Washington **appointed**, or chose, the heads of these departments. Two of them were especially important. One was the **secretary of state**. This is the person in charge of America's foreign policy. The other was the **secretary of the treasury**. This is the person in charge of collecting, managing, and spending the government's money. Washington chose Thomas Jefferson for his secretary of state. He chose Alexander Hamilton for his secretary of the treasury. Washington's other advisors were Secretary of War Henry Knox and Attorney General Edmund Randolph.

PRESIDENTIAL PORTRAIT

John Adams (1735–1826)

Second president of the United States
Vice president: Thomas Jefferson
Term: 1797–1801
Party: Federalist
Home state: Massachusetts

John Adams was a leader in the Revolutionary War. He was also one of the signers of the Declaration of Independence. His family was the first to live in the newly built White House.

PRACTICE 18: Washington and His Cabinet

Circle the letter of the correct answer to each of the following questions.

1. Who was George Washington's vice president?
   - **a.** Edmund Randolph
   - **b.** John Adams
   - **c.** Alexander Hamilton
   - **d.** Thomas Jefferson

2. How many departments made up the first cabinet?
   a. two
   b. three
   c. four
   d. fourteen

3. What are the responsibilities of the secretary of state?
   a. collect, manage, and spend the government's money
   b. appoint the other members of the Cabinet
   c. answer all letters and calls to the president
   d. carry out America's foreign policy

THINK ABOUT IT

George Washington's Cabinet had four departments. Today, the Cabinet is made up of these 15 departments:

State
Treasury
Defense
Justice
Interior
Agriculture
Commerce
Labor
Health and Human Services
Housing and Urban Development
Transportation
Education
Energy
Veterans' Affairs
Homeland Security

Why do you think there are so many more advisors today than there were in Washington's time? Write your answer on a separate sheet of paper.

Jefferson and Hamilton

Thomas Jefferson and Alexander Hamilton were both members of Washington's Cabinet. Even though they had to work together, Jefferson and Hamilton did not always agree. Each had his own ideas about how the Constitution should be **interpreted**, or understood. For example, they disagreed over how much power the national government should have.

Jefferson believed that the common people should have a part in running the government. He did not want to give power to the federal government at the expense of the states. Jefferson feared that a very strong central government would lead to tyranny. **Tyranny** is when one person rules and does not consider the needs and wishes of the common people. Jefferson believed in an **agrarian** (farming) society. This would be made up of independent farmers and small tradesmen.

Thomas Jefferson

Hamilton favored a strong central government and less power for the states. He did not believe that the common people were able to govern themselves wisely. Instead, he wanted a government run by the educated, wealthy classes of people. Hamilton felt that giving the common people too much voice in government would lead to mob rule. Hamilton also supported the development of shipping and manufacturing.

Differences like these about the new government led to the rise of political parties. A **political party** is a group of people who share the same ideas about government. Each party has its own ideas about how the government should be run. Today, the two major political parties are the Democratic Party and the Republican Party. In the early days of government, Hamilton led the **Federalist Party**, and Jefferson led the **Democratic-Republican Party**.

Alexander Hamilton

Federalists admired British society and government. They shared Hamilton's fear of mob rule. Democratic-Republicans admired the new revolution in France. They thought Federalists wanted a return to rule by a king or queen.

■ PRACTICE 19: Jefferson and Hamilton

Below is a list of citizens. Based on what you have just read about the beliefs of Thomas Jefferson and Alexander Hamilton, decide which man each citizen would have supported. Write Jefferson (**J**) or Hamilton (**H**) on each blank.

_____ **1.** a farmer

_____ **2.** a rich businessman

_____ **3.** a manufacturer who exports to Europe

_____ **4.** a carpenter working for a shipbuilder

UNIT 1 REVIEW

Circle the letter of the correct answer to each of the following questions.

1. Why did the English troops take over Boston, Massachusetts?
- **a.** It was the only place that had homes in which the troops could stay.
- **b.** Many colonists there had spoken out against English rule.
- **c.** The colonists had shot some English soldiers near the State House.
- **d.** Boston had the port closest to England.

2. What caused the Boston Tea Party?
- **a.** England was getting back at the colonies for the Boston Massacre.
- **b.** England forced the colonists to use one tea company.
- **c.** England blocked Boston Harbor.
- **d.** General George Washington ordered the colonists to start a battle.

3. What did the Treaty of Paris do?
   a. set the boundaries of the new country
   b. recognized the 13 states as free and independent
   c. both *a* and *b*
   d. neither *a* nor *b*

4. What was the purpose of the Second Continental Congress?
   a. to write the Constitution
   b. to ratify the Articles of Confederation
   c. to set up a federal government
   d. to declare war on England

5. Which of the following was a major reason why the Articles of Confederation did not work?
   a. They gave more power to the states than to the federal government.
   b. The settlers in the 13 states came from different parts of Europe.
   c. Each state already had a governor.
   d. all of the above

6. What was the most important issue at the Constitutional Convention?
   a. whether amendments should be added to the Articles of Confederation
   b. how to divide power between the states and the federal government
   c. how to set up a system of taxation
   d. whether to count slaves as part of the population

7. Why did the delegates at the Constitutional Convention decide that tax bills would come from the House of Representatives?
   a. to please states with large populations
   b. to please all the slave states
   c. to please the states on the East Coast
   d. to please states with small populations

8. Who holds concurrent powers?
   a. the federal government
   b. the state governments
   c. both the federal government and state governments
   d. individual citizens

9. Who is in the Cabinet?
   a. the heads of the government's executive departments
   b. the heads of the state governments
   c. the president
   d. anyone who advises the president

10. Which of the following did Thomas Jefferson fear?
   a. a strong central government that would get too strong
   b. a cabinet that was not elected by the common people
   c. mob rule, in which the common people had too much say in government
   d. none of the above

UNIT 1 APPLICATION ACTIVITY 1

The Explorers

Explorers are those who travel to places where few people have ever been before. Throughout history, explorers have traveled on foot, by boat, by plane, by spaceship, or even on the back of a four-footed animal. The names of some famous explorers are listed below.

Marco Polo	Meriwether Lewis	Sir Francis Drake
Vasco da Gama	William Clark	Matthew Henson
Erik the Red	Sacagawea	Roald Amundsen
Leif Eriksson	Captain James Cook	Louise Arner Boyd
Mary Kingsley	Osa Johnson	Ibn Battuta
Christopher Columbus	Ferdinand Magellan	Isabella Eberhardt

Choose three explorers from the list on page 43. Using an encyclopedia and/or the Internet, research the journeys of these three explorers. Take notes on a separate sheet of paper.

Now, find a copy of a world map. Locate the starting place and ending place of each explorer's journey on the map. Then, label each point with the explorer's name, the year or years of the trip, and his or her means of transportation. An example would be *Captain Cook, 1768, by ship.* If the explorer made more than one trip, choose the one that most interests you.

Optional Activity: Of the three explorers you chose, which one would you have liked to be? Imagine you are that explorer during one of his or her trips. On a separate sheet of paper, write a journal entry that you might have written during the trip. As you write, think about where you are exploring, what type of land, plants, and animals surround you, and when in history your trip is taking place.

UNIT 1 APPLICATION ACTIVITY 2

Find the Connections

Look at the five circles below. Each of these five presidents took part in the founding of the United States. There were many connections between them. For example, John Adams was a member of the committee of the Continental Congress. This group wrote the Declaration of Independence. Thomas Jefferson was the chairman of that committee. The line between the two presidents shows that link.

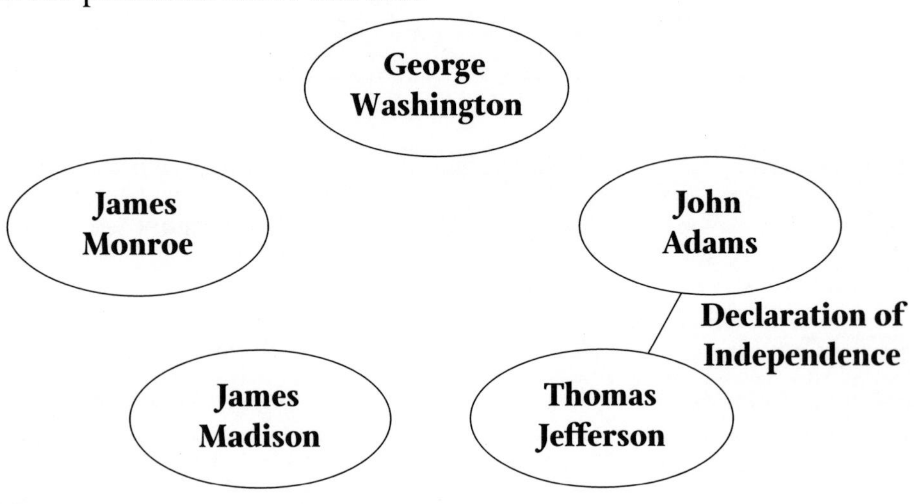

Research each of the five presidents. Use an encyclopedia, a biographical dictionary, and/or the Internet. Take notes on the major activities of each man during and after the American Revolution. Look for what these men had in common. When you find a link, draw a line between the circles and label it.

Below are some possible connections:

- Continental Congress
- Constitutional Convention
- served in the Revolution
- served as his vice president
- came from Virginia
- was a member of his Cabinet

UNIT 1 APPLICATION ACTIVITY 3

Wanted: A Secretary of State

As you have learned, Thomas Jefferson was the first secretary of state. Here are some of the other people who have held this job: William H. Seward (secretary of state to Abraham Lincoln), Cordell Hull (secretary of state to Franklin D. Roosevelt), Madeleine Albright (secretary of state to William Clinton), and Condoleezza Rice (secretary of state to George W. Bush).

Use the library or the Internet to find out the main responsibilities of the secretary of state. Then, think of the kind of qualifications or background a person needs to make a good secretary of state. Take notes on the lines below.

____

____

____

____

____

____

____

A president must carefully make the choice of who to name as secretary of state. A select group of people is considered for the position. Imagine, though, that this job was advertised in your local newspaper, just like any other job. What would the ad say? Using the notes you took on page 45, write a want ad for the position of secretary of state. You may want to look at a few want ads in your local newspaper for style ideas. Use the lines below to create your ad.

WANTED

UNIT 2

Development of the Nation I

LESSON 5: Westward Expansion

GOAL: To identify the causes, events, and results of the westward expansion of the United States

WORDS TO KNOW

Alamo	**Lone Star Republic**	**nomadic**
annex	**Louisiana Purchase**	**Northwest Territory**
California Gold Rush	**Manifest Destiny**	**Oregon Country**
Canal Era	**merchant vessels**	**prospector**
Forty-niners	**Mexican Cession**	**reservation**
free state	**migration**	**Seward's Folly**
frontier	**Missouri Compromise**	**territory**
Gadsden Purchase	**Monroe Doctrine**	**Treaty of Ghent**
Homestead Act	**nationalism**	**War of 1812**
homesteader	**neutral**	**westward expansion**

Westward Expansion

In 1800, the population of the United States was a little over 5 million. These people lived in .9 million square miles along the Atlantic coast. However, it did not take long for America to start growing. Throughout the 1800s, the American frontier moved west. A **frontier** is a boundary between land that is settled and land that is unsettled. As settlers moved farther west, the frontier kept moving with them.

By 1900, the United States controlled much more **territory**, or land. The country's land area had grown from .9 million to 3 million square miles. The population had also greatly increased. By 1900, there were 75 million people living in America. Less than half of these people lived in the original 13 states. New lands were settled as the nation spread across the continent.

Look at the map below. This map shows all of the new territories gained by the United States in the 1800s. You can refer to this map throughout this lesson.

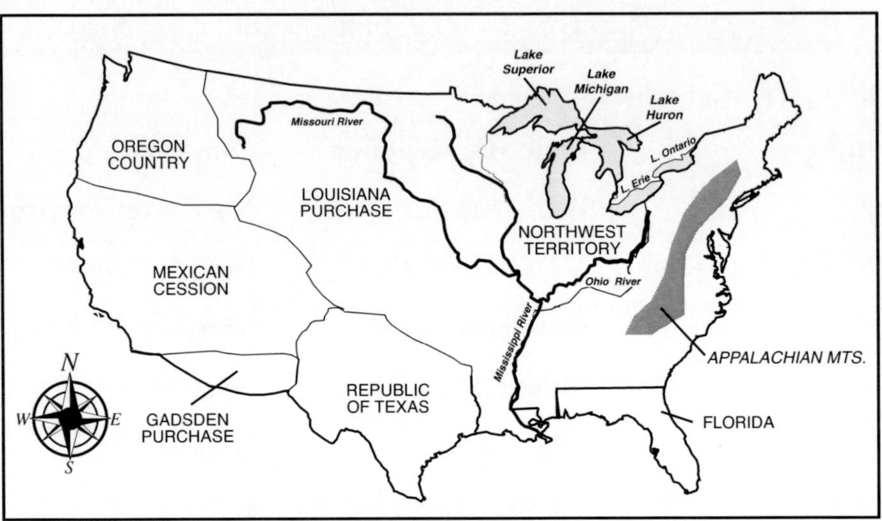

This lesson explains the **westward expansion**, or growth toward the west, of the United States. It also examines the nation's development into a world power.

The Northwest Territory

Expansion of the New World started soon after the colonies gained independence from England. Settlers began to head west. They rushed to the frontier, looking for good farmland and a chance to make it on their own. Between 1791 and 1796, the United States added three more states to its union: Vermont in 1791, Kentucky in 1792, and Tennessee in 1796.

Then, the nation began expanding into the **Northwest Territory**. This was the land northwest of the original 13 states. It was given to America as part of the Treaty of Paris in 1783. Today, this area is known as the Midwest. Once this area was settled, new states were established. Ohio was admitted as a state in 1803. Illinois, Indiana, Michigan, and Wisconsin became states in the years that followed.

THINK ABOUT IT

Most people think of western settlers as traveling in covered wagons. However, many families traveled down the Ohio River on flatboats. A flatboat was a huge raft made of heavy planks. All of the family's possessions were loaded onto the flatboat. This included their farm animals, which were tied to the rear of the boat. What do you think were some advantages of traveling in flatboats? Write your answer on a separate sheet of paper.

PRACTICE 20: The Northwest Territory

Circle the letter of the correct answer to each of the following questions.

1. What is a frontier?

- **a.** a place where a battle is fought
- **b.** a boundary between settled and unsettled lands
- **c.** a growing population
- **d.** a border between two states

2. Which of the following states was NOT part of the Northwest Territory?

- **a.** Vermont
- **b.** Ohio
- **c.** Michigan
- **d.** Illinois

Threats of War

Soon after the American Revolution ended, the people of France began their own revolution. The new French government declared war on England and other nations in Europe. The United States had promised to help France in case of war. But the country was too small and too weak to do so at the time. The United States could not afford another war. So, it decided to stay **neutral**. This meant that it did not side with either England or France.

The Americans continued trading with both of the warring nations. This was risky. It meant that American **merchant vessels**, or trade ships, shared the seas with warships from England and France. Both English and French warships tried to stop American ships from reaching their enemy's ports. England did not want Americans to sell France supplies that might help France win the war. France felt the same way about American ships reaching English ports. Therefore, both countries began attacking American ships.

This made the Americans very angry. It looked as though war could break out with both countries. However, the United States signed a treaty with England in 1794. England agreed to remove its warships from the northeast coast of the United States. The United States also signed a treaty with France.

More and more, the United States realized it would have to be strong to get along in the world.

■ PRACTICE 21: Threats of War

Decide if each statement below is true (**T**) or false (**F**). Write the correct letter on the line before each statement.

______ **1.** If a country remains neutral in a war, it joins forces with the weaker country.

______ **2.** Americans continued to trade with both England and France while the two countries were at war with each other.

______ **3.** America had to pay a fine to England if it wanted to trade with France.

The Louisiana Purchase

The next problem for the United States involved the Mississippi River. Settlers in the Northwest Territory used the Ohio and Mississippi rivers to get their farm goods to markets in the East. These rivers were the only way for farmers to move their crops. There were very few roads. And the roads that did exist were useless for heavy loads.

The Mississippi River was also very important because it emptied into the Gulf of Mexico. The river met the Gulf at the port of New Orleans.

In New Orleans, goods that had traveled down the river could be loaded onto ocean ships. These ships could then travel to the Atlantic Ocean and to important ports in Europe. In 1802, Americans were told by France that they could no longer use the port of New Orleans. France owned this area and the millions of acres of land west of the Mississippi known as Louisiana.

Thomas Jefferson was the U.S. president at this time. He decided to try to buy New Orleans from France. The French leader, Napoleon, agreed to sell the land. He needed the money to pay for France's war with England.

America bought New Orleans and the entire Louisiana Territory in 1803. This was a total of 500 million acres. This price was 15 million dollars. At 3 cents per acre, this was a great deal! Known as the **Louisiana Purchase**, it nearly doubled the size of the United States.

PRESIDENTIAL PORTRAIT

Thomas Jefferson (1743–1826)

Third president of the United States
Vice president: James Madison
Term: 1801–1809
Party: Democratic-Republican
Home state: Virginia

Jefferson is probably best remembered for something he did years before he became president. This was writing the Declaration of Independence. Once he was president, one of Jefferson's most important acts was the Louisiana Purchase. Jefferson also sent Meriwether Lewis and William Clark on America's first overland expedition. Lewis and Clark traveled all the way to the Pacific Ocean in 1801. Jefferson was a well-educated man. He is remembered not only as a statesman but also as a scientist, an educator, and a philosopher.

PRACTICE 22: The Louisiana Purchase

Circle the letter of the correct answer to each of the following questions.

1. Why did Napoleon agree to sell the Louisiana Territory?

a. He did not want to own land in North America.

b. He needed money to pay for France's war with England.

c. He knew that the Louisiana Territory had poor land for farming.

d. He wanted to help the Americans.

2. Why was New Orleans such an important port?

a. It allowed farmers in the Northwest Territory to trade goods with Mexico.

b. It allowed farmers in the Northwest Territory to reach the Atlantic Ocean and ports in Europe.

c. It allowed farmers in the East to send goods to the Northwest Territory.

d. It was the only port in the United States at the time.

TIP

Maps can help you learn about history as well as geography. For example, look back at the map on page 50. Note that the Northwest Territory is *east* of the Louisiana Purchase. You already know that the United States was settled in a *westward* movement. This should tell you that the Northwest Territory was probably settled *before* the Louisiana Purchase land.

The War of 1812

Peace between America, France, and England did not last long. England and France started fighting again. When this happened, both countries went back to capturing American ships trying to reach their ports. This time, the United States stopped trading with both nations. However, losing this trade hurt the United States more than it hurt England or France.

There was also a second problem between the United States and England. England did not want American settlers to continue moving westward. They did not want the United States to become larger or more powerful. So, the English backed the Native Americans in their ongoing fight against American settlers. Native Americans were also against the settlers' westward movement. More and more Native Americans were being pushed out of their lands and homes as settlers moved west. The English helped the Native Americans fight against these American settlers.

In the summer of 1812, President James Madison declared war on England. Most Americans did not want to go to war. They wanted to keep the peace. They did not believe that America was ready for another war.

PRESIDENTIAL PORTRAIT

James Madison (1751–1836)

Fourth president of the United States
Vice president: James Monroe
Term: 1809–1817
Party: Democratic-Republican
Home state: Virginia

As you have learned, James Madison is often called the Father of the Constitution. He had the leading role in writing that important document. Before becoming president, Madison served in Congress. He also was secretary of state under President Thomas Jefferson. The War of 1812 was the most significant event of Madison's presidency. At one point, Madison and his family even had to flee the White House as the British invaded Washington, D.C. Madison's wife, Dolley, was a graceful and popular hostess. Dolley Madison was one of the best-loved first ladies in American history.

This new war with England was called the **War of 1812**. It was fought in many battles along the border between Canada and the United States. To many people's surprise, the Americans were able to fight off the

English. They regained control of the Great Lakes. Yet, the Americans did not do as well as they had hoped. For one thing, they had tried to invade and conquer Canada, but they failed.

The **Treaty of Ghent**, signed in 1814, ended the War of 1812. It restored all borders to where they had been before the war. However, none of the issues that had led to war were solved. Neither country gained any territory. But, it was the last time that England and the United States were on opposite sides in a war.

IN REAL LIFE

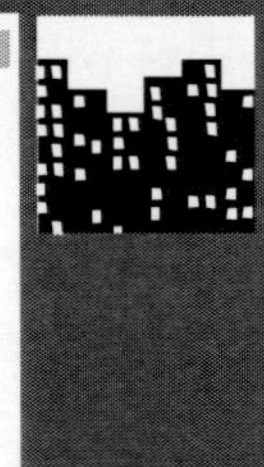

It may be hard for you to imagine what it felt like to be a soldier during the 1800s. Reading the words to "The Star-Spangled Banner" may give you some idea. This song was written by Francis Scott Key during a battle in the War of 1812. He was on a British ship and watched the entire battle. Even though he wrote the famous song in 1814, it did not become America's national anthem until 1931.

PRACTICE 23: The War of 1812

Circle the letter of the correct answer to each of the following questions.

1. Why did America declare war on England in 1812?
- **a.** to stop England from attacking American ships
- **b.** to stop England's involvement in the battles between settlers and Native Americans
- **c.** to invade and conquer Canada
- **d.** all of the above

2. Who won the War of 1812?
- **a.** America
- **b.** England
- **c.** France
- **d.** no one

Growing Nationalism

One result of the War of 1812 was a growing feeling of national pride, or **nationalism**. Americans finally felt that they belonged to one nation. Instead of feeling loyal to their individual states, Americans felt loyal to the nation as a whole. After the war, people turned their attention to settling the West. America continued to expand its boundaries. Its population grew, too. Many new settlers came to the United States from Europe, which was finally at peace.

The postwar years (the years after the war) saw the growth of industry and manufacturing. Americans also began developing faster ways to travel. For example, new roads and canals were built. The Erie Canal was built in New York during this time. Started in 1817, this waterway took eight years to build. When it was finished, it provided an all-water route from New York to the Great Lakes.

Now, people, goods, and ideas were able to move from one part of the country to another quickly and easily. As a result, more and more of the population moved westward. Communities developed along the Great Lakes and the Mississippi and Ohio rivers. Territories soon had enough people to become states.

IN REAL LIFE

Today, people are amazed at how quickly goods, people, and ideas can travel from one part of the country to another. Fax machines, overnight mail services, the Internet, high-speed trains, and faster cars allow people to travel and communicate more quickly than ever before. Back in the early 1800s, canals were just as amazing. So many canals were built between 1825 and 1840 that people call this time the **Canal Era**. When the 363-mile-long Erie Canal was finished in 1825, it was possible to go by boat from New York to the Great Lakes in only ten days! For the 1800s, this was incredible timing. Today, of course, the same trip takes less than a day.

PRACTICE 24: Growing Nationalism

Check each statement below that is TRUE.

- ☐ **1.** After the War of 1812, Americans felt more loyal to their own states than to the country as a whole.
- ☐ **2.** Industry and manufacturing grew in the years after the War of 1812.
- ☐ **3.** After the War of 1812, more Americans moved westward.

The Florida Purchase and the Monroe Doctrine

In the early 1800s, Florida was controlled by Spain. It was used as a hideout by pirates, smugglers, runaway slaves, and a group of Native Americans called Seminoles. These people were unfriendly to settlers. For example, the Seminoles would raid southern settlements, then retreat into Florida. The United States could not do anything once the raiders were in Florida, because it was under Spain's control.

In 1818, General Andrew Jackson led a military force into Florida. He crushed the Seminoles and captured two Spanish forts. Spain decided to sell Florida to the United States before it was captured. This way, they would at least get paid for it. In 1819, Secretary of State John Quincy Adams arranged for the United States to pay Spain 5 million dollars for Florida.

By now, Europe was beginning to respect the United States. In 1823, President Monroe made it clear that Europe and the Americas were separate, and were to stay that way. Monroe told the rest of the world that the United States would not interfere in European affairs. He also said that Europe should not interfere in the affairs of any countries in either North or South America. This policy came to be known as the **Monroe Doctrine.** Its purpose was to prevent European nations from further colonizing the Western Hemisphere.

PRESIDENTIAL PORTRAIT

James Monroe (1758–1831)

Fifth president of the United States
Vice president: Daniel D. Tomkins
Term: 1817–1825
Party: Democratic-Republican
Home state: Virginia

Before he became president in 1817, Monroe served as a senator, minister to France, and secretary of state (under President James Madison). As president, Monroe was known for the Florida Purchase and the Monroe Doctrine. He was also famous for managing the **Missouri Compromise** in 1820. This agreement allowed Maine to enter the United States as a free (non-slaveholding) state, while Missouri entered as a slaveholding state. The Missouri Compromise prevented any states north of 36° 30' north latitude from being slaveholding states. Monroe also supported the return of black slaves, brought against their will to the United States from Africa, to the new nation of Liberia. The capital of Liberia is named Monrovia after President Monroe.

PRACTICE 25: The Florida Purchase and the Monroe Doctrine

Circle the letter of the correct answer to each of the following questions.

1. Who were the Seminoles?

- **a.** a group of Native Americans who resented American settlers
- **b.** pirates from South America
- **c.** American settlers who lived in Florida
- **d.** English soldiers

2. Why did Spain decide to sell Florida to the United States?
    a. It needed the money to pay for a war.
    b. It no longer wanted to own land in North America.
    c. Florida did not have good land for farming.
    d. It was afraid that it would lose all of Florida by force.

3. What was the purpose of the Monroe Doctrine?
    a. to stop Spanish attacks on America
    b. to prevent Europe from interfering with the Americas
    c. to keep the United States from getting involved in Europe
    d. both *b* and *c*

THINK ABOUT IT

The Monroe Doctrine stated that the United States would not interfere in any of Europe's affairs. Today, however, many people consider the United States to be the "policeman of the world." This means that the United States has a responsibility to interfere wherever human rights are in danger. Do you think the United States should interfere in the affairs of other countries? Or, do you think every country should be left to do as it chooses? Why? Write your answer on a separate sheet of paper.

Manifest Destiny

By the 1840s, the population of the United States had increased to nearly 20 million. America had grown from the 13 colonies to a nation that was able to stand up to the rest of the world.

New inventions, such as steamships, railroads, and telegraph lines, were improving the lives of many Americans. America had developed into a world power. It was a united and strong nation that could influence other countries around the globe.

This power made many Americans believe that the United States should expand its territory all the way to the Pacific Ocean. They believed that the United States, as a world power, had the right to continue its growth. Many felt this right was given to them by God. This belief became known as **Manifest Destiny**. Manifest Destiny was the idea that westward movement was both necessary and good in the eyes of God.

THINK ABOUT IT

As settlers moved westward, they took over land already occupied by Native Americans. As you have learned, this made the Native Americans very angry. Often, they would refuse to leave and would instead fight for the land. Imagine that you have been asked to help these two groups work out their differences. What kind of compromise might you offer? Write your answer on a separate sheet of paper.

PRACTICE 26: Manifest Destiny

Decide if each statement below is true (**T**) or false (**F**). Write the correct letter on the line before each statement.

______ **1.** The population of the United States was about 20 million by the 1840s.

______ **2.** Manifest Destiny was the belief that God gave the United States the right to expand westward.

______ **3.** America was losing its strength as a world power by the 1840s.

America Moves Toward the Pacific Ocean

At first, the United States could not expand into Texas. Texas was part of Mexico, which was owned by Spain. In 1821, however, Mexico became its own nation. All of Spain's land west of the Mississippi River then became the property of Mexico. This land included Texas.

The Mexicans were eager to settle Texas. They invited Americans to come as settlers. In return, the Americans promised to obey the laws of Mexico and belong to the Catholic Church.

Over 30,000 American settlers had come to Texas by 1836. The Mexican government began to feel frightened that the American settlers would take over Texas. So, they said that no more Americans could come to Texas. This angered the settlers, who rebelled.

On March 2, 1836, the American settlers in Texas decided to declare Texas an independent nation. Mexican leader Santa Anna led an army to fight the Texans. An early battle took place at the **Alamo**, an old Spanish mission, or church, in San Antonio, Texas. The battle went on for 11 days. In the end, the Mexicans defeated the Texans and killed all 187 settlers defending the church.

The Alamo

American General Sam Houston was the commander in chief of the Texan army. On April 21, he led 800 furious American Texans in another battle at San Jacinto. Houston's battle cry was "Remember the Alamo!" When the battle was over, Mexico was defeated and Texas was a free nation. It became known as the **Lone Star Republic.** It chose Sam Houston as its first president.

Even though Texas wanted to join the United States at once, it was not accepted as a state until 1845. The delay was due to a disagreement between southern slave states and northern anti-slavery states. The northern states did not want Texas to become a state because slavery was allowed in Texas. The southern states were in favor of Texas becoming a state, because this would give the slave-holding South more political power. U.S. politicians also worried that another war with Mexico would break out if Texas became part of the United States.

Eventually, America realized that it was better to have Texas as a state than to worry about other nations (such as France or England) attacking the small republic. President James Polk encouraged Congress to **annex,** or add, Texas to the United States. The Lone Star Republic became the Lone Star State in 1845. Once more, America grew in size.

PRESIDENTIAL PORTRAIT

James K. Polk (1795–1849)

Eleventh president of the United States
Vice president: George M. Dallas
Term: 1845–1849
Party: Democratic
Home state: Tennessee

Just under 50 years old, James Polk was the youngest president up to that time. He had practiced law in Tennessee and was a popular political speaker. Once in politics, Polk rose quickly to a position of power. His career was furthered by his wife, Sara Childress Polk. For 25 years, she served as his close companion and advisor. Polk had a difficult time as president, partly due to bitter divisions between the states in Congress. Historians view him as a capable and just president. Exhausted by his duties, Polk died only three months after the end of his term.

PRACTICE 27: America Moves Toward the Pacific Ocean

Match each term on the left with a description on the right. Write the letter of the correct description on the line before each term.

_____ **1.** the Alamo	**a.** a Mexican leader who led the Mexican army in battle at the Alamo
_____ **2.** Sam Houston	**b.** the name for Texas after it declared its independence from Mexico
_____ **3.** James Polk	**c.** the president of the United States during the time that Texas became a state
_____ **4.** Santa Anna	**d.** the commander in chief of the Texan army
_____ **5.** the Lone Star Republic	**e.** an old Spanish mission in San Antonio where the Mexican army defeated a group of Texans

The Mexican War

The Mexicans were very angry when they heard that the United States was going to make Texas a state. When Texas became a state, Mexico declared war on the United States. The United States probably would not have agreed to go to war if Texas had been the only issue. But, President Polk also wanted to buy the Mexican territories of California and New Mexico.

In the summer of 1846, General Zachary Taylor led his American troops to the first victories of the Mexican-American War. These occurred near the Rio Grande. In the meantime, American forces also won parts of California. Settlers declared this territory the Republic of California. American troops then captured the California cities of Monterey, San Francisco, and Santa Fe. By the end of 1847, American troops had also pushed southward all the way to Mexico City. This is still the capital of Mexico. The United States now had control over most of the Southwest.

General Zachary Taylor

THINK ABOUT IT

Zachary Taylor became the twelfth president of the United States in 1849. For most of his life, Taylor had been a soldier. He was one of many presidents who first won fame as soldiers. George Washington and Andrew Jackson are two other examples. Why do you think that so many former soldiers were elected president? Write your answer on a separate sheet of paper.

The Mexican-American War ended in February 1848. In the treaty that was signed, Mexico agreed to give up all of Texas. It also handed over all of its territory from the border of the Louisiana Purchase to the Pacific Ocean. This included California and most of what is now New Mexico. The United States agreed to pay 15 million dollars for this territory, which became known as the **Mexican Cession**. The southern border of the United States was now the Rio Grande.

Five years later, the United States paid Mexico another 10 million dollars. This time, it was for some land in southern Arizona and New Mexico. This action was called the **Gadsden Purchase.** The purchase of this land marked the end of continental expansion in the United Sates.

PRACTICE 28: The Mexican War

Circle the letter of the correct answer to each of the following questions.

1. Why did President Polk decide to go to war with Mexico?

- **a.** He wanted to buy California and New Mexico.
- **b.** He was afraid Mexico would capture Florida.
- **c.** He wanted to buy Texas from Mexico.
- **d.** none of the above

2. What area did America gain during the Mexican War?

- **a.** the Northwest
- **b.** the Northeast
- **c.** the Southeast
- **d.** the Southwest

3. What was the Mexican Cession?

- **a.** the treaty that ended the Mexican War
- **b.** the first battle of the Mexican War
- **c.** the land Mexico sold to America right after the Mexican War
- **d.** the land Mexico kept after the Mexican War

4. How much did America pay for the Gadsden Purchase?

- **a.** 3 million dollars
- **b.** 10 million dollars
- **c.** 15 million dollars
- **d.** 30 million dollars

Oregon Country

During the Mexican-American War, the United States had also added another piece of land to its territory. This land was known as **Oregon Country**. It was located in the northwestern part of North America.

Both the United States and England had owned parts of the Oregon Country. People from both nations had settled in the area. In 1846, England offered to divide the territory into two nearly equal parts. The northern half would belong to England. The southern half would go to the United States. President Polk agreed to this offer.

Because of this bargain with England, America's Manifest Destiny was complete. The United States reached from the Atlantic Ocean to the Pacific Ocean. Now came the most difficult challenge—settling the frontier.

IN REAL LIFE

Do you ever wonder how events—such as parades, marathons, and other gatherings—get their names? Think about the events that take place in your town or city. Most likely, some of these events were named after a particular person or place. Events have been named this way for many years. The Treaty of Paris is one example. Another example is the Gadsden Purchase. James Gadsden was an American soldier who helped the government complete the Gadsden Purchase. Although James Gadsden has been pretty much forgotten, his name lives on in history because of this purchase.

PRACTICE 29: Oregon Country

Circle the letter of the correct answer to each of the following questions.

1. Which territory completed America's Manifest Destiny?

- **a.** the Oregon Country
- **b.** Texas
- **c.** California and New Mexico
- **d.** Florida

2. How did the United States and England end their conflict over the Oregon Country?
   a. England took all of it.
   b. The United States took all of it.
   c. It was given to France.
   d. Both countries split it.

Settling the Frontier

As you have learned, the United States expanded greatly in the 1800s. Yet, most of the population remained on the East Coast. Between the settled lands in the East and the coast of California, there were huge stretches of available land. Most of this land was now claimed by the U.S. government.

In 1862, the government passed the **Homestead Act**. It was meant to encourage people to move west and set up farms on these lands. Under this act, the U.S. government agreed to give a 160-acre plot to any homesteader. A **homesteader** is a person who is willing to take over land and build a home on it.

Getting to the frontier was not easy. Groups started out with packed wagons and high hopes. The trip would prove to be dangerous, exhausting, and seemingly endless. Once there, life on the frontier was difficult. People had to work hard and help one another. Farmers and ranchers who settled the plains endured winter blizzards and summer droughts (periods of very dry weather). They were often faced with swarms of plant-eating insects. Outlaws attacked, robbed, and killed people. Finally, there was the struggle with Native Americans, who lived on these plains first.

However, settling the frontier was important to Americans. For many, it was an escape from overcrowded eastern cities and factory jobs. The land in the plains was also fertile and good for growing crops. Railroads made it easier for people to travel west. Railroads helped western farmers send their produce back for sale in the East, too.

■ PRACTICE 30: Settling the Frontier

Decide if each statement below is true (**T**) or false (**F**). Write the correct letter on the line before each statement.

_____ **1.** The U.S. government wanted Americans to settle the new territories in the West.

_____ **2.** The Homestead Act was passed to encourage settlers to remain in eastern cities.

_____ **3.** Life on the frontier was difficult.

_____ **4.** Many Americans moved west to escape crowded cities in the East.

_____ **5.** Under the Homestead Act, western farmers were not allowed to do business with markets in the East.

The Rush for Silver and Gold

In 1848, gold was discovered near San Francisco, California. Within months, this news had spread throughout the nation and the world.

As a result, there was a huge **migration** (move) westward. This migration was called the **California Gold Rush**. During 1849 alone, 80,000 prospectors looking for gold and silver made their way to California. (A **prospector** is someone who goes to search for mineral riches because of the prospect, or hope, of finding it.) The prospectors came by land and by sea. For a time, it seemed that everyone was going to California. The trouble was, these people only wanted to hunt for gold. Very few wanted to grow food or build houses.

The trip to California was not easy. A trip by covered wagon took months or even a year. To travel by water, a person had to sail around South America. This usually took four months. Still, California grew.

By 1850, California had a large enough population to become a state. It entered the United States as a **free state.** This was the term used for states that did not allow slavery.

TIP

You may have heard the term **Forty-niners.** This was the name given to gold prospectors who traveled by sea to California. Remembering this name can help you remember the year of the California Gold Rush—18**49**.

About ten years later, more gold and silver were found in Colorado, Nevada, and the Dakotas. Whenever gold or silver was found, thousands of prospectors would rush to the area. Towns grew overnight. However, these towns emptied out as soon as the mining was over.

In 1867, Secretary of State William Seward bought the Alaska Territory for 7.2 million dollars. Many Americans thought that Seward had made a big mistake. They thought he had paid too much money for what they saw as a cold, empty, useless piece of land. They called it **Seward's Folly** (foolishness). Then, gold was discovered in Alaska in 1896. People changed their minds about Seward's decision. Many rushed to the area. In 1959, Alaska became a state.

PRACTICE 31: The Rush for Silver and Gold

Match each term with its description below. Write the letter of the correct term on the line before each description.

a. Alaska **b.** Forty-niners **c.** prospector **d.** free state

_____ **1.** someone looking for gold

_____ **2.** Seward's Folly

_____ **3.** a state that does not allow slavery

_____ **4.** people who traveled by sea to California in hope of finding gold

The Indian Wars

As you have learned, Native Americans were the earliest Americans, living in the territory of the United States long before European explorers arrived. The colonists took over the land and established the 13 colonies. The Native Americans, called Indians by the colonists, were forced either to live under the colonists' new rules or to leave.

At that time, many Native Americans led **nomadic** lives. This meant that they moved around from place to place. As American settlements continued to expand, Native Americans were driven farther west.

In 1862, Native Americans living on the plains between the Mississippi River and the Pacific Coast joined together and attacked the U.S. settlements. The settlers then attacked Native American settlements. These attacks became known as the Indian Wars.

In 1867, the U.S. government set up two reservations for the Native Americans. A **reservation** is land reserved, or set aside, for one purpose. But, the Native Americans were used to a nomadic life. They did not want to become farmers. So, the fighting continued.

In 1874, gold was discovered in the Black Hills of North Dakota, part of a reservation for the Sioux tribe. Prospectors came to the area. In June 1876 chiefs Crazy Horse and Sitting Bull gathered 2500 Sioux near the Little Bighorn River. They planned to fight against the U.S. government and its policy of white settlement on their land. On June 25, General George Custer and his troops attacked the Native Americans in their camp. The Sioux, in the Battle of Little Bighorn, defeated Custer and killed over 200 soldiers.

But the Sioux were fighting a losing battle, faced with a military power they could not defeat. They also saw that they could not stop the Americans' westward expansion. A transcontinental railroad was being built to make the West easier to reach. In 1886, Geronimo, leader of the Apaches (a Native American tribe in the Southwest), was captured. After that, most Native American nations of the West gave up and agreed to settle on reservations.

Geronimo

TIP

You cannot always look up words you do not know. In many cases, you can guess the meaning of a word by reading the words around it. When you gather clues about a word's meaning from the words around it, you are looking at *context clues.* For example, find the word *transcontinental* in the last paragraph. If you do not know what this word means, you can get a good idea by looking at the other words in the sentence. It says that the *transcontinental* railroad was being built to *cross* the country. *Transcontinental* is a word that describes something that goes across a continent.

PRACTICE 32: The Indian Wars

Circle the letter of the correct answer to each of the following questions.

1. What is a reservation?

- **a.** any state in the West that was occupied by Native Americans
- **b.** a Native-American attack on an American settlement
- **c.** land set aside for a special purpose
- **d.** a railroad system

2. Why were Native Americans opposed to settling in reservations?

- **a.** They were used to moving from place to place.
- **b.** They did not want to be farmers.
- **c.** both *a* and *b*
- **d.** neither *a* nor *b*

3. Who was Geronimo?

- **a.** a leader of the Apaches, a Native American tribe in the Southwest
- **b.** chief of the Sioux Indians
- **c.** an American general who killed many Native Americans
- **d.** none of the above

LESSON 6: The Civil War and Reconstruction

GOAL: To identify the causes, events, and results of the U.S. Civil War

WORDS TO KNOW

abolitionists
agricultural
black codes
blockade
Civil War
Confederate States of America
economy
Emancipation Proclamation
Fifteenth Amendment
Fourteenth Amendment
Freedmen's Bureau
Gettysburg Address
impeach
industrial
invasion
Ku Klux Klan
nullify
plantations
Radicals
Reconstruction
Republican Party
secede
servitude
siege
sovereignty
stalemate
suffrage
tariffs
Thirteenth Amendment
Yankees

Conflicts Between North and South

Throughout the early 1800s, the United States grew in many ways. The size of the nation expanded as new lands were added. The population increased, as did the country's **economy**, or sources of wealth. As the nation developed, however, different areas developed in different ways. The northern states had many factories. The southern states had many large farms. As a result, the two regions had different interests. There were three major areas of conflict between the North and the South: trade laws, sovereignty, and slavery.

Trade Laws

The economic differences between the North and South meant that each region had different needs. The northern states were **industrial**. This means that goods were produced in factories throughout the North. The northern states felt threatened by America's trade with England. English goods were cheaper than those produced in the North. The northern states worried that Americans would buy English goods instead of American goods. This would hurt northern industries. To protect American industries, Congress passed trade laws that placed **tariffs**, or taxes, on imported goods (goods shipped from other countries to the United States). To avoid this tariff, Americans would buy more goods produced in America. This helped northern industries.

However, the southern states had fewer industries. The South was mainly **agricultural**, or based on farming. The largest of these farms were called **plantations**. Southern states wanted to be able to buy England's cheaper goods. They were against the trade laws passed by Congress. The southern states declared that they would **nullify**, or cancel, these laws.

Sovereignty

Sovereignty was another conflicting issue between the South and the North. **Sovereignty** means the supreme, or absolute, power of a territory.

The southern states believed that state governments should have sovereignty in all political matters. This meant that the federal government would not be able to tell states what to do. The North, however, believed that the federal government should have sovereignty over states. Northerners felt that the United States would be strong only if the central government had the highest power. They felt that the United States would break up if each state could choose which laws it wanted to obey.

Slavery

The issue of slavery was another area of conflict between the North and the South. The agricultural economy of the South depended on the labor of slaves. The slaves were people whose ancestors had been captured in Africa, or who had been captured in Africa themselves. They were brought to this country and sold to southern plantation owners and others. The southern states wanted new states to allow slavery. Many northerners, however, felt that it was wrong for one person to "own" another. They wanted to stop the spread of slavery.

Those who believed that slavery was wrong were called **abolitionists.** They wanted to abolish, or end, slavery. Abolitionists went on speaking tours to tell people that slavery was wrong. They formed anti-slavery societies and published books, pamphlets, and newspapers opposing slavery. They called on Congress to free all slaves. However, southern representatives in Congress would not allow it.

Slaves in a Cotton Field

CIVIL WAR PORTRAIT

Frederick Douglass (1817–1895)
Writer, speaker, newspaper editor
Birthplace: Baltimore, Maryland

Frederick Douglass was one of the most famous African American abolitionists. He was born a slave in Maryland. As a child, Douglass was one of the few slaves who was taught to read. In 1838, Douglass escaped slavery. He did this by dressing up as a sailor. With forged papers, he made his way to New York and became free. Douglass soon became one of the most powerful leaders of the abolitionist movement.

PRACTICE 33: Conflicts Between North and South

Circle the letter of the correct answer to each of the following questions.

1. Why did the North and South have different interests in the 1800s?

- **a.** because they were ruled by separate governments
- **b.** because people in the North came from England, and people in the South came from other European countries
- **c.** because the North was mainly industrial, and the South was mainly agricultural
- **d.** none of the above

2. What is sovereignty?

- **a.** a state that does not allow slavery
- **b.** a person who speaks out against slavery
- **c.** trade between states
- **d.** the supreme power of a territory

3. Which of the following statements is TRUE?

- **a.** Southern states supported a strong central government.
- **b.** Southern states opposed trade laws that placed tariffs on imported goods.
- **c.** Most northern states wanted to keep slavery.
- **d.** Northern states supported the sovereignty of states.

4. What was an abolitionist?

- **a.** an escaped slave
- **b.** a southern governor
- **c.** a person who spoke out against slavery
- **d.** a person who spoke out in favor of slavery

THINK ABOUT IT

Former slaves who had escaped to the North often worked as abolitionists. They knew firsthand how terrible slavery was. Many northern abolitionists encouraged former slaves to speak out. Why do you think it was important to have former slaves share their stories with the public? Write your answer on a separate sheet of paper.

The Union Splits

In 1854, a new political party was formed. It was called the **Republican Party**. One of the party's main ideas was to stop slavery in the new territories of the United States. In 1860, Republican candidate Abraham Lincoln was elected president of the United States. Lincoln strongly believed that slavery was wrong.

Several southern states had declared that they would **secede**, or break away, from the United States if Abraham Lincoln became president. By February 1, 1861, seven southern states had withdrawn from the United States. They were South Carolina, Mississippi, Florida, Alabama, Georgia, Louisiana, and Texas. These seven states formed a separate nation called the **Confederate States of America**. This nation had its own constitution. It elected Jefferson Davis as its president.

Jefferson Davis

President Lincoln asked the seven states to come back into the United States. He promised to allow them to keep slavery. However, they refused. Lincoln did not believe that any state had the right to secede. He promised to do all that he could to save the United States, even if it meant war.

PRACTICE 34: The Union Splits

Circle the letter of the correct answer to each of the following questions.

1. Abraham Lincoln belonged to which of the following political parties?
- **a.** Democratic
- **b.** Republican
- **c.** Federalist
- **d.** Democratic-Republican

2. Which of the following states did NOT break away from the United States in 1861?
   a. Maryland
   b. Texas
   c. Alabama
   d. Mississippi

3. What was the Confederate States of America?
   a. the states occupied by slaves who escaped from the South
   b. the southern states that supported Abraham Lincoln
   c. the group of states that remained part of the United States
   d. the states that broke away from the United States to form a new union

The Civil War Begins

The nation was divided. The differences in opinion between the South and the North were too great to overcome. As a result, the two sides went to war—the newly formed Confederate States of America (or Confederacy) versus the Union (the other United States). This war became known as the **Civil War**.

Once it formed, the Confederacy began seizing U.S. property in the South. On April 12, 1861, Confederate forces started firing on Fort Sumter in Charleston, South Carolina. The fort was a U.S. military post manned by U.S. soldiers. This attack on Fort Sumter started the Civil War.

When the war began, four more states quickly joined the Confederacy. They were North Carolina, Tennessee, Arkansas, and Virginia. The mountainous part of Virginia did not like slavery, so it broke away and became West Virginia. West Virginia stayed with the United States and became a separate state in 1863. The slave states of Missouri, Kentucky, Maryland, and Delaware also remained part of the United States. This meant that the North had 23 states on its side. The South only had 11. The map on the next page shows the Confederacy at the start of the Civil War.

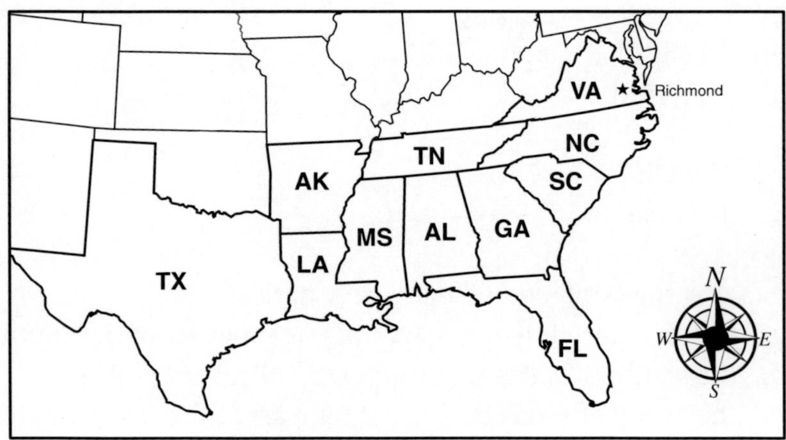

Confederate States of America

The North had about 22 million people living in its territory. The South had only about 9 million. Over 3 million of these people were slaves, who were not allowed to fight. The North had more factories, better transportation, an army, a navy, and the federal government. As a result, many northerners were sure that the war would be over in a few days.

However, the Confederate states did have some advantages. They had good military leaders. Many of their men were experienced soldiers or hunters. Also, most of the war was fought on southern land. Thus, the Confederates were fighting on, and defending, their own territory. Like the northerners, most Confederates expected a swift, easy victory as the war began.

President Lincoln quickly called for 75,000 volunteers to fight the South. Soon, the new Union army marched toward the Confederate capital at Richmond, Virginia.

The Confederate army met the Union army near Richmond. To many people's surprise, the well-trained Confederate soldiers defeated the Union soldiers. At this point, people realized that the Civil War might last longer than expected.

The Civil War became a long, bloody, and bitter struggle. It divided not only the nation but families, too. Often, brothers, fathers, and sons fought on different sides. No matter which side won, the wounds would take a long time to heal.

PRESIDENTIAL PORTRAIT

Abraham Lincoln (1809–1865)

Sixteenth president of the United States
Vice president: Andrew Johnson
Term: 1861–1865
Party: Republican
Home state: Illinois

Abraham Lincoln was president during the Civil War. He felt that the war was necessary to save the Union. A great speaker and writer, his ability to understand military strategy helped the North win the war.

PRACTICE 35: The Civil War Begins

Decide if each statement below is true (**T**) or false (**F**). Write the correct letter on the line before each statement.

_____ **1.** The Civil War began when the United States split and the two sides went to war against each other.

_____ **2.** During the war, several slave states remained part of the Union.

_____ **3.** The Confederacy was much larger than the Union.

_____ **4.** Abraham Lincoln became the first president of the Confederacy.

_____ **5.** The Confederacy had a strong army because many slaves were experienced soldiers.

_____ **6.** Most of the Civil War was fought in the North.

_____ **7.** The capital of the Confederacy was Richmond, Virginia.

_____ **8.** After the first battle, many people realized that the Civil War was going to be a long, bitter struggle.

THINK ABOUT IT

Many people think that the Civil War was only about slavery. Yet, the issue of sovereignty was also at the heart of the war. As you have learned, the North believed that there should be a sovereign central government. The South wanted each state to have individual sovereignty. What are some advantages and disadvantages of a sovereign central government? What might be some advantages and disadvantages of individual state sovereignty? Write your answer on a separate sheet of paper.

Major Battles of the Civil War

The Civil War lasted from 1861 to 1865. By the end of the war, nearly 618,000 people had been killed. Nearly 400,000 more had been wounded. In the following section, you will learn about some of the major battles of this war.

Bull Run

You have already learned about the first battle of the Civil War. This battle became known as the Battle of Bull Run. The Union army simply was not ready for this battle. Its commanders had had too much confidence. Some people treated the battle almost as a sporting event. They traveled from nearby Washington, D.C., bringing picnic lunches. They came to watch what they thought would be an easy and final northern victory. Instead, they saw the Confederate army defeat the Union army in a brutal battle.

IN REAL LIFE

Have you ever thought that it was going to be easier to solve a problem than it actually was? Have you ever found yourself without enough time or help to complete a task? This happens to people all the time. Even President Lincoln made this mistake. Lincoln thought he would need about 75,000 volunteers to defeat the Confederate army. Before the war was over, 4 million men had fought in the Union army.

Antietam

From 1861 until 1863, the war was at a **stalemate.** This means that neither side was winning. The Union and Confederate armies met several times. The Confederates won several important battles. But, their victories were not great enough to discourage the **Yankees** (a name given to the northerners by the South).

A turning point came when Confederate General Robert E. Lee led an **invasion,** or attack, on Maryland in September 1862. He hoped the people of Maryland would rise up and support the Confederate army. Instead, the battle of Antietam was one of the bloodiest battles of the war. Nearly 5,000 soldiers were killed and more than 18,000 were wounded. The Confederate army was forced out of Maryland by the Union army. This was a key development for the northern forces. Still, there were huge casualties on both sides.

CIVIL WAR PORTRAIT

Robert E. Lee (1807–1870)

Commander of the Confederate forces
Home state: Virginia

Robert E. Lee came from a military family. His father, "Light-Horse Harry" Lee, had been a hero in the Revolutionary War. Robert E. Lee graduated from West Point in 1829. Lee freed his own slaves. He was also against the South's separation from the United States. Lee was offered command of the Union army. However, he refused it and resigned from the U.S. army. When his home state seceded, he felt he had to join the Confederate forces. Lee was admired by both northerners and southerners for his skills, bravery, and dignity.

New Orleans, Shiloh, and Vicksburg

One of the quickest ways to divide the South was to take control of the Mississippi River. To do this, David Farragut took a fleet of Union ships to New Orleans in 1862. As you have learned, New Orleans is a major port city at the end of the Mississippi River. Farragut's fleet defeated the Confederate ships guarding the city. Thus, he captured New Orleans.

Meanwhile, Union General Ulysses S. Grant had captured several forts in Tennessee. His armies moved south toward Mississippi. Confederate forces met Grant at Shiloh, a town in Tennessee. Grant had not expected the Confederate attack. At first, it seemed that the Union army would be defeated. Then, more Northern troops arrived, and Grant defeated the southerners.

After resting, Grant's army marched to Vicksburg, Mississippi. Grant surrounded the Confederate fort in this town and began a long siege. In a **siege,** an army surrounds an area and waits for the other side to surrender. On July 4, 1863, Vicksburg surrendered. This gave the North control of the Mississippi River. Arkansas, Texas, and Louisiana were cut off from the rest of the South.

Ulysses S. Grant

Chancellorsville and Gettysburg

Meanwhile, General Joseph Hooker led the Union Army in an effort to cut General Lee off from Richmond, Virginia. Lee came out to meet Hooker in Virginia's wilderness. He defeated Hooker at Chancellorsville, but each side lost more than 10,000 men.

After the battle at Chancellorsville, Lee invaded Pennsylvania. He hoped to pressure the North on its own territory. This attack led to the great battle at Gettysburg, a town in Pennsylvania. In 1863, General George G. Meade met General Lee at Gettysburg for a four-day battle. When the fighting ended, Lee had lost the battle. He had to escape with his army into Virginia. A total of 50,000 soldiers from both sides were killed or reported missing at Gettysburg.

President Lincoln came to Gettysburg after the battle to open a large military cemetery. He dedicated the cemetery to those killed in battle.

His short speech, known as the **Gettysburg Address**, is still one of the most moving speeches ever made. In this speech, he honored the men who died at Gettysburg. Lincoln expressed his hope that the nation would "have a new birth of freedom—and that government of the people, by the people, for the people, shall not perish from the earth."

CIVIL WAR PORTRAIT

Clara Barton (1821–1912)
Nurse, founder of the American Red Cross
Birthplace: Oxford, Massachusetts

Clara Barton nursed the wounded during the Civil War. The soldiers named her the Angel of the Battlefield. In addition to serving the wounded, she also helped northern families look for their sons who were missing in action. Later, in 1881, Barton went on to found the American Red Cross.

Sherman's March

In May 1864, Union General William T. Sherman left Tennessee with 100,000 troops. His plan was to march south from Tennessee to Atlanta, Georgia. This would split the Confederacy in half. Then, he would march from Atlanta to the Atlantic Ocean. This would cut the supply line between the western and eastern parts of the Confederacy. Meanwhile, the Union navy had set up a **blockade** along the east coast of the Confederacy. It was stopping, or blocking, all ships from entering or leaving Confederate ports.

General William T. Sherman

Sherman's 300-mile march through Atlanta to the ocean is remembered for its terrible destruction. He and his troops burned and destroyed many buildings, homes, farms, and railroads along the way.

■ PRACTICE 36: Major Battles of the Civil War

Circle the letter of the correct answer to each of the following questions.

1. Who won the Battle of Bull Run?
  a. the Confederate army
  b. the Union army
  c. both *a* and *b*
  d. neither *a* nor *b*

2. Where did the Battle of Antietam take place?
  a. Pennsylvania
  b. Virginia
  c. Mississippi
  d. Maryland

3. What is a *siege*?
  a. a bloody battle
  b. the surrounding of an area
  c. a peaceful agreement
  d. a type of rifle

4. Which of the following statements about the Battle of Gettysburg is TRUE?
  a. It lasted ten days.
  b. The Confederate army defeated the Union army.
  c. It was started by General Lee and the Confederate army.
  d. Very few people died in this battle.

5. Who gave the Gettysburg Address?
  a. President Abraham Lincoln
  b. the mother of a lost soldier
  c. General Joseph Hooker
  d. Clara Barton

6. Where did General William Sherman lead his troops in 1864?
  a. from Tennessee to Atlanta (Georgia), then to the Atlantic Ocean
  b. from Kentucky to Richmond, Virginia
  c. from Virginia to Pennsylvania, then to the ocean
  d. none of the above

The South Surrenders

By 1865, the war was nearing an end. It was clear that both the Union army and the Confederate army had skilled generals and soldiers. But, the Union army had more soldiers and supplies than the Confederate army.

In the spring of 1865, General Ulysses S. Grant captured the Confederate capital at Richmond, Virginia. He went on to trap the Confederate army and asked the South to surrender. Confederate General Robert E. Lee finally agreed. The surrender took place in the Virginia town of Appomattox Court House. At last, the Civil War was over. The states were again united.

Sadly, the surrender was not the end of deaths due to the Civil War. Five days after Appomattox, President Lincoln and his wife went to the Ford Theater in Washington, D.C. President Lincoln was shot while watching the play. He died early the next morning. His murderer, John Wilkes Booth, was unhappy about the defeat of the South. People in both the North and South mourned the death of the president. Without Lincoln's leadership, rebuilding the nation would be much harder.

PRACTICE 37: The South Surrenders

Decide if each statement below is true (**T**) or false (**F**). Write the correct letter on the line before each statement.

_____ **1.** The North won the Civil War.

_____ **2.** After the Civil War, the Confederacy became an independent nation.

_____ **3.** The Civil War ended in 1865.

_____ **4.** President Lincoln was killed before the Civil War ended.

_____ **5.** John Wilkes Booth was vice president of the United States during the Civil War.

After the War

There were two major results of the Civil War. First, the power of the federal government was established. States did not have the right to nullify laws or to secede. Second, all slaves were freed, and slavery was outlawed in the United States.

During the war, President Lincoln had issued a statement called the **Emancipation Proclamation.** This document proclaimed, or declared, that slaves in the South were emancipated, or free. This document was issued in 1863. However, it could only go into effect if the North won the war. When the North won the Civil War in 1865, southerners were forced to grant freedom to all their slaves. Soon after, Congress passed the **Thirteenth Amendment** to the Constitution. This amendment abolished (ended) **servitude**, or slavery, in the United States.

The Emancipation Proclamation did not free slaves in the South until after the war. It did, however, result in one major change before the war was over. The Emancipation Proclamation encouraged many African Americans to join the Union Army. About ten percent of all Union volunteers were free African Americans or escaped slaves. In all, about 185,000 African American soldiers served in the Union army. Many other African American volunteers helped the north as sailors, hospital workers, laborers, and even as spies.

Twenty African American soldiers received the Congressional Medal of Honor. This is the government's highest award for bravery. Over 65,000 African American volunteers died in the Civil War.

■ PRACTICE 38: After the War

Circle the letter of the correct answer to each of the following questions.

1. Which of the following was NOT a result of the Civil War?
   a. The power of the federal government was established.
   b. State governments were given absolute power.
   c. All slaves were freed.
   d. Slavery was outlawed in the United States.

2. When did President Lincoln write the Emancipation Proclamation?
   a. before the Civil War
   b. during the Civil War
   c. the day the Civil War ended
   d. after the Civil War

TIP

You may be interested in learning more about the Civil War. Perhaps there is a specific topic that has really caught your interest—such as the role of women or African Americans in the war. Or, maybe you would like to know more about the types of weapons or ships used in the Civil War. One way you can learn more about a specific topic is to research it on the Internet. There are many Internet sites that focus on the Civil War. One is the U.S. Civil War Center, at **http://www.cwc.lsu.edu**. This site offers links to many other Civil War sites. If you would like to see photographs of the Civil War, you can check out **http://memory.loc.gov/ammem/cwphtml/cwphome.html.**

Reconstruction

The period after the Civil War is known as **Reconstruction.** To *reconstruct* means to rebuild. Before President Lincoln died, he had already started making plans to rebuild the divided nation. He did this to encourage the southern states to get their state governments working again quickly. Railroads, roads, bridges, and farms in the South would have to be repaired or rebuilt. Most importantly, the people of the nation needed to learn to live in peace.

Andrew Johnson became president after Lincoln's assassination. Johnson was faced with many problems. He tried to follow the plans Lincoln had made for rebuilding the South. Unfortunately, he was not a strong leader. Congress disagreed with many of Johnson's policies. It would not let him put his plans to work.

Many of the Republicans in Congress were abolitionists. They wanted to be sure that the rights of African Americans in the South would be protected. Johnson, on the other hand, felt that the future of African Americans should be left in the hands of southern leaders.

Then, southern states began passing the so-called **black codes.** These laws were meant to limit the rights of African Americans. Therefore, the **Radicals,** a group of Republicans in Congress, helped pass two amendments to the Constitution. These were designed to protect the rights of African Americans.

One of these was the **Fourteenth Amendment,** passed in 1868. This amendment guarantees civil rights to all citizens, including former slaves. The second was the **Fifteenth Amendment,** passed in 1870. This amendment declares that **suffrage,** or the right to vote, cannot be denied on account of race, color, or previous slavery. This meant that former male slaves now had the right to vote. (No women had the right to vote in the United States until the Nineteenth Amendment was passed in 1920.)

In addition to these amendments, Congress set up the **Freedmen's Bureau.** The purpose of this bureau, or department, was to help former slaves get food, housing, and education. At first, this bureau worked well. Over time, though, it was taken over by dishonest people. It soon lost its usefulness.

PRESIDENTIAL PORTRAIT

Andrew Johnson (1808–1875)

Seventeenth president of the United States
Vice president: none
Term: 1865–1869
Party: Republican
Home state: North Carolina

Congress thought that Andrew Johnson favored the South. They went so far as to **impeach** him. That is, they accused him of misconduct, or improper behavior, while he was in office. Johnson was tried in court and found not guilty.

In spite of laws and amendments, African Americans in the South did not hold on to their new rights for long. Some white southerners formed groups that used terror to regain white control. For example, some former soldiers joined a secret organization called the **Ku Klux Klan.** Members of the Klan gathered at night disguised in white robes and hoods. They rode through the country frightening, and often killing, African Americans. Soon, the Klan was feared throughout the South. Its tactics prevented most African Americans from voting.

Reconstruction ended in 1872. Yet, southern African Americans did not fully recover their civil rights until the 1960s. In fact, problems between the North and the South remained important issues in American politics. The United States was one nation again. In many ways, however, it was still divided.

PRACTICE 39: Reconstruction

Match each term below with the correct description. Write the letter of the term on the line before each description.

a. Reconstruction **b.** Fourteenth Amendment **c.** Fifteenth Amendment

d. suffrage **e.** Freedmen's Bureau **f.** Ku Klux Klan

_____ **1.** This is the right to vote.

_____ **2.** This is the period after the Civil War.

_____ **3.** This gave former male slaves the right to vote.

_____ **4.** This secret group, formed by white southerners, used terror to gain white control.

_____ **5.** This guarantees civil rights to all citizens of the United States.

_____ **6.** This department was set up by Congress to help former slaves get food, housing, and education.

UNIT 2 REVIEW

Circle the letter of the correct answer to each of the following questions.

1. How did the United States gain the Northwest Territory?
   a. in a war with Mexico
   b. as part of the Treaty of Paris
   c. in a war with Canada
   d. by buying it from France

2. Which of the following statements describes the Louisiana Purchase?
   a. It nearly doubled the land area of the United States.
   b. America had to fight a war to get it.
   c. Spain sold the land to the United States.
   d. all of the above

3. Why did England capture American ships before the start of the War of 1812?
   a. to steal American weapons
   b. to steal American goods
   c. to destroy American ships
   d. to prevent America from trading with France

4. What was the purpose of the Erie Canal?
   a. to provide an all-water route from New York to the Great Lakes
   b. to connect the Great Lakes to the Mississippi River
   c. to allow western farmers to reach the port of New Orleans
   d. to connect the Atlantic and Pacific oceans

5. What message did the Monroe Doctrine send to European countries?
   a. The United States would establish colonies in Europe.
   b. Europe could not establish colonies anywhere in the world.
   c. Europe could not establish any new colonies in the Americas.
   d. The United States would govern South America.

6. Why did the Native Americans eventually agree to settle on reservations?
  a. They knew they could never defeat the American army.
  b. The transcontinental railroad allowed more and more people to move west.
  c. Geronimo, the leader of the Apaches, was captured.
  d. all of the above

7. What advantage did the South have in the Civil War?
  a. most of the manufacturing and railroad lines
  b. a larger population
  c. experienced military leaders
  d. a majority of the states

8. What advantage did the North have in the Civil War?
  a. a larger population and a majority of the states
  b. help from England
  c. the chance to fight on its own territory
  d. both *a* and *c*

9. What did the Emancipation Proclamation do?
  a. It ended the Civil War.
  b. It freed all the slaves in the South.
  c. It allowed slavery to continue in the South.
  d. It added an amendment to the Constitution.

10. Which of the following guaranteed suffrage for all former slaves?
  a. the black codes
  b. the Fourteenth Amendment
  c. the Freedmen's Bureau
  d. the Fifteenth Amendment

UNIT 2 APPLICATION ACTIVITY 1

These Honored Dead

President Abraham Lincoln gave the Gettysburg Address in November 1863. He gave the speech on the battlefield in Gettysburg, Pennsylvania, to dedicate the Soldiers National Cemetery. Lincoln spoke only ten sentences, but his powerful words became some of the most famous of all time. Many people do not know that another person gave a speech just before Lincoln that day. His name was Edward Everett. He spoke for two hours, but his words were overshadowed by Lincoln's.

Imagine that you are the person chosen to speak before Lincoln. You are to greet the audience and introduce President Lincoln. You may want to say something about the following:

- why people are gathered there
- how honored you are to be making the introduction
- the president's role in the Union
- some details about the Battle of Gettysburg

Write your speech on the lines below.

Introduction to the Gettysburg Address

UNIT 2 APPLICATION ACTIVITY 2
On the Trail

Thousands of settlers headed west on the Oregon Trail during the 1840s and 1850s. The first wagon train of settlers reached Oregon by this trail in 1842. For the next ten years, more and more people followed.

Imagine that you are a settler traveling on the Oregon Trail. On your journey, you meet some travelers who are headed in the opposite direction. They offer to deliver any letters you have written to your family and friends back home. You decide to write a letter about your experiences on the Oregon Trail.

In your letter, describe what you have seen along the way. Have you met any other people? What animals have you seen? Has it been easy to get food and to stay warm? What problems have you had? How much farther do you have to travel?

Write your letter on the lines below.

Dear ____________________,

____

____

____

____

____

____

____

____

____

____

____

____

UNIT 2 APPLICATION ACTIVITY 3

Point of View

There are two sides to every battle. Most likely, the people on each side will have their own opinion about how a battle was fought. The same is true of battles in the Civil War. Union soldiers and Confederate soldiers probably felt very differently about each battle.

Here are some of the major battles of the Civil War:

- Bull Run (First Battle), July 1861
- Shiloh, April 1862
- Bull Run (Second Battle), August 1862
- Antietam, September 1862
- Chancellorsville, May 1863
- Gettysburg, July 1863
- Vicksburg, July 1863

Choose one of the battles from the list above. Work with a partner who is interested in the same battle. Decide which side each of you will be on. If you are a Union soldier, your partner should be a Confederate soldier. Together, use encyclopedias and/or the Internet to learn all you can about the battle you have chosen.

Next, role-play a conversation with your partner, imagining you are these two soldiers. Talk about your experiences in the battle. Try to make your conversation as real as possible.

After you have finished your conversation, think about your two opinions of the same battle. What did you disagree about? What did you agree on? On the lines on page 95, explain how you and your partner agreed and/or disagreed about the battle.

UNIT 3

Development of the Nation II

LESSON 7: Industrialization and Urbanization

GOAL: To identify the causes, events, and results of industrialization and urbanization in the United States in the late 1800s

WORDS TO KNOW

child labor	**loom**	**suburbs**
commuter	**mass production**	**technology**
conveyor belt	**mill**	**textile**
factory towns	**omnibus**	**unions**
geography	**raw materials**	**urban centers**
Industrial Revolution	**reform movements**	**urban transportation**
interchangeable parts	**sanitation**	**urbanization**

The Industrial Revolution

The Industrial Revolution in the United States began in about 1770 and continued through the 1800s. Usually, a revolution suggests a war. However, it can also mean a great change. The **Industrial Revolution** is the term used for the era when human and animal power shifted to machine power. The changes brought about by the Industrial Revolution were not only great but long-lasting. Before 1770, skilled craftspeople made things mainly by hand. They often worked on a product from start to finish. For example, **textile** workers, who made cloth, would spin cotton and wool into thread. Then, they would weave the thread into cloth. They worked in their own homes or in small shops.

Then came a time of great inventiveness. Clever people invented one machine after another. For example, scientists discovered that steam was a source of power. It could be used to power boats and trains. It was also applied to (used in) the building of machinery for factories. The use of this and other scientific knowledge in industry is called **technology**.

The Industrial Revolution actually started in England. The English were careful to guard their technology secrets. In fact, English people who knew these secrets were not allowed out of the country. Then, American businessmen started offering cash prizes for cloth-making machines. An Englishman named Samuel Slater heard of the prizes. Slater was in charge of making machinery for an English cotton **mill**, or factory. He secretly left the country and came to the United States. In 1790, Slater built a machine in the United States that spun thread. To build it, Slater used only his memory of the machine he had left behind. This was one of America's first factory machines. Slater then built America's first textile mill. The mill was built in Pawtucket, Rhode Island, next to a waterfall. At that time, factories depended on rapidly (fast) flowing water to turn the huge wheels that drove the machinery.

The machine built by Slater spun thread out of cotton and wool. Now, the Americans needed a machine that would weave the thread into cloth. This is called a **loom**. The first power looms in America were built by a Boston merchant named Francis Cabot Lowell. He hired an expert to build and install the looms in a Waltham, Massachusetts, mill.

The changes Slater brought from England helped usher in the Industrial Revolution in the United States. In the textile industry and in many other industries, much of the labor done by humans and animals would soon be done by machines.

PRACTICE 40: The Industrial Revolution

Circle the letter of the correct answer to each of the following questions.

1. What is a revolution?

- **a.** a time of great change
- **b.** a period of no change
- **c.** a disagreement between people
- **d.** a small change

2. When did the Industrial Revolution occur in the United States?
    a. from the early 1600s to the mid-1700s
    b. from the early 1700s to the mid-1800s
    c. from the late 1700s through the 1800s
    d. from the late 1800s through the 1900s

3. What happened to the U.S. textile industry during the Industrial Revolution?
    a. It moved from the factory into the home.
    b. More and more craftspeople wove cloth by hand.
    c. Machines started doing work that people used to do by hand.
    d. It moved to England, where there was more advanced technology.

Urbanization

During the Industrial Revolution, many thousands of people moved into towns where factories were located. Those towns quickly grew into cities. They became **urban centers**. The process of people moving to the cities, and the growth of these cities, is called **urbanization**.

There are two key reasons for the urbanization that happened during this period. First, factory machines started doing the work that craftspeople once did. Machines could do the work faster and at less cost. As more and more factories sprang up, many craftspeople found it hard to make a living. They could not compete with the efficiency of factory production. So, many craftspeople left their small towns and villages to work in the factories. More and more people moved to work in **factory towns**. These were towns in which almost everyone worked in the factories. Most of the other people in the town depended on the factories, too. They ran shops and businesses that were used by factory workers.

A second reason for the urbanization of this period was new farming technology. One machine could do the work of several people and could do it faster. Therefore, not as many farmworkers were needed to produce the same amount of food. The machines were more efficient than the farmworkers. With this more efficient farm machinery, many farmworkers lost their jobs. They, too, came to the cities to try to find jobs as factory workers.

Why did cities develop in certain parts of the United States and not in others? **Geography** was the main reason. Geography involves the location and physical features of an area. During the Industrial Revolution, geography often determined which areas were good locations for factories. Factories were usually opened in areas that were near four things:

- a source of **raw materials**, or goods, needed to make a final product
- a source of power
- markets in which the goods could be sold
- a means of transportation

First, being near a source of raw materials was one way for a factory to be efficient. This helped the factory save money and time. For example, a cloth factory would need cotton to make its cloth. So, it might be located in the southern part of the United States, where much of the country's cotton was grown.

Second, being near a source of power was also efficient. If a factory used steam power, it needed a source of wood or coal to burn to produce the steam. If it used water power, a factory needed to be near a river.

Third, being near markets was also efficient. For example, a cloth factory might be close to where cloth merchants set up their stores. Or, it might be near another factory that made items out of the cloth.

Finally, being near a river, road, or railroad (or, later, a canal) was also efficient. These transportation routes made it easier to ship finished goods to merchants or other factories.

Any location that provided all four of these things was a good place to set up a factory. Other factories would follow. Workers would follow the new jobs. Housing would be built for the workers and their families. Businesses would spring up to provide goods and services to the factory owners and working families. Soon, there would be a new city spreading in all directions.

PRACTICE 41: Urbanization

Decide if each statement below is true (**T**) or false (**F**). Write the correct letter on the line before each statement.

_____ **1.** Urbanization is the process of people moving to cities and those cities growing larger.

_____ **2.** Many craftspeople could no longer make a living because they could not compete with factory machines.

_____ **3.** Farmworkers were not affected by the Industrial Revolution.

_____ **4.** Most factory towns were built in areas that had raw materials, good transportation, nearby markets, and power sources.

Important Inventions

As you have learned, two important inventions of the Industrial Revolution were spinning and weaving machines. The work of these machines was faster and cheaper than human labor.

Perhaps the most important invention of the Industrial Revolution was the steam engine. The steam engine was developed in England. It channeled the force of steam to provide power. Steam-powered engines were much more efficient than water-powered machines. They also did not require that a factory be located near a river or waterfall.

By 1802, Oliver Evans of Delaware had steam-powered engines driving the machines in his flour-making mill. He went on to build steam-powered engines for other manufacturers. Evans is also responsible for the invention of the **conveyor belt**. This is a belt that moves materials and products from one part of a factory to another. Modern-day factories still use conveyor belts.

Another important development of the Industrial Revolution was the idea of **interchangeable parts**. This idea was developed by Eli Whitney, a manufacturer of muskets (guns). Whitney thought that having one person build a musket from start to finish was not efficient. Each part would fit only in that one musket. Whitney thought it would be more efficient if each worker made just one part of the gun and did it the same way each time. Then, other workers would put those parts together. Because the parts were always made the same way, they would always fit together correctly. This idea worked especially well with metal parts. Soon, Europeans were coming to America to learn this way of doing things.

Each new invention started a process that led to other ideas, other inventions, and more changes. The 1800s saw the development of a process for mass-producing steel. **Mass production** means making things in large amounts and for less money. Steel was used to build railroad rails and bridges that were strong enough to carry heavy engines, also made of steel. Improved transportation made it possible to get raw materials from distant places. Manufacturers could now ship finished products almost anywhere.

The mass production of steel, along with the invention of elevators, made taller buildings a possibility. Cities could build upward as well as sideways. Then cities began to build electrical systems in the 1880s.

Inventions in communication were also key factors of the Industrial Revolution. The telegraph was invented in 1844. The typewriter came along in 1867. The first telephone call was made in 1876. All of these inventions made communication easier and businesses more efficient.

A Time Line of Firsts

1765	steam engine
1765	spinning machine
1807	successful steamboat trip
1814	steam locomotive
1844	telegraph
1846	sewing machine
1858	transatlantic telephone cable
1861	elevator
1866	dynamite
1867	typewriter
1869	U.S. transcontinental railroad
1878	lightbulb
1890	fountain pen
1891	refrigerator
1892	diesel engine
1892	clothes dryer

PRACTICE 42: Important Inventions

Check each statement below that is TRUE.

☐ **1.** The steam engine was one of the most important inventions of the Industrial Revolution.

☐ **2.** Steam-powered engines were not as efficient as the waterpower used before.

☐ **3.** Interchangeable parts meant that one person would build each machine, from start to finish.

☐ **4.** The telegraph, telephone, and typewriter were all important inventions of the Industrial Revolution.

IN REAL LIFE

You have just read about the incredible number of machines developed during the Industrial Revolution. This was one of the most dramatic periods of change in history. Some people believe that the "computer revolution" has been almost as dramatic. Think about the ways in which computers have changed life for people since the 1980s. Computers are now used in offices, factories, hospitals, and service industries. They are used to monitor the thermostat in people's houses, to run cars, and to total purchases at the grocery store. With computers, you can bank, shop, and find information without ever leaving your home. Can you think of any other ways in which computers affect your life?

Problems of the Cities

The new factory cities grew so quickly that there was no time to plan them carefully. Many problems came with this fast growth. For example, there was not enough housing. Large families sometimes lived in small, crowded spaces. **Sanitation** was also a problem. That is, it was hard to keep the cities clean and healthy. The growing cities simply did not have the equipment needed to take care of the large numbers of people who arrived so suddenly.

The factories themselves were usually large and often noisy, dirty, and dangerous. Workdays were long and hard. There were no laws requiring regular breaks or lunch hours. There was little time to rest. Still, workers had to be careful not to get their clothes or hands caught in the machinery. Many workers were badly hurt or even killed. A tired worker could easily get careless.

Life in the factory was entirely new for the workers. Farmworkers, for example, were used to long hours and hard work. However, they were also used to fresh air and sunlight. Craftspeople were used to putting their own ideas into their work. Now, they just made whatever the factory owner told them to make. There were no short breaks for chatting with neighbors or friends. That could not happen until the long day was over.

Life in the city was difficult, too. Some city dwellers lived next door to factories. Factories could be noisy and smoky. Often, factories released waste products into local streams or rivers.

So many people lived in the cities that no one had much space or land. Also, there were few places where people could go to enjoy themselves, such as parks. This was especially difficult for people who had come from the countryside.

■ PRACTICE 43: Problems of the Cities

Decide if each statement below about the Industrial Revolution is true (**T**) or false (**F**). Write the correct letter on the line before each statement.

_____ **1.** Large families often lived in small, crowded rooms.

_____ **2.** Cities were kept clean and safe.

_____ **3.** The government made sure that factory workers worked in safe, healthy conditions.

_____ **4.** Many workers were hurt, and even killed, after getting their hands or clothes caught in machinery.

Urban Transportation

In the early 1800s, most city dwellers had to walk to work. Therefore, the cities stayed small and compact (packed together). This all changed with the introduction of **urban transportation.** This is transportation in a city that is available to the public for a fare (fee). Examples of urban transportation include trolleys, buses, and subways.

An early form of urban transportation was the horse-drawn **omnibus.** People could ride in these vehicles for a small price. (The word *bus* comes from this early form of transportation, the omni*bus*.) The first streetcars, which ran on rails, were also drawn by horses. Then came electrification in the 1880s. Along with the streetcars, there were now trolleys that got their power from wires that ran overhead. Elevated railways (also called "els") appeared in New York in the 1870s. Because these els were noisy and ugly, other cities put their trains underground and called them *subways.* Special trains that made several short, local stops also appeared. They were called commuter trains. A **commuter** is a person who commutes, or travels, between home and work.

Urban transportation made it possible for people to work in the city without living there. People who could afford to started to move farther outside the city, creating suburbs. **Suburbs** are the areas that surround an urban center. The suburbs sprang up in what had been the countryside. Where once there had been farms or woods, now there were neighborhoods of homes. Houses were built farther apart than in the city, and people had more space. As people continued to move to the suburbs, more and more of the countryside started disappearing. The face of America was changing.

PRACTICE 44: Urban Transportation

Decide if each statement below is true (**T**) or false (**F**). Write the letter of the correct answer on the line before each statement.

_____ **1.** People have always been able to commute from the suburbs to the city.

_____ **2.** Some early forms of urban transportation included horse-drawn omnibuses and streetcars.

_____ **3.** The areas outside a city where people live are called urban centers.

_____ **4.** As urban transportation took hold, fewer and fewer people moved out to the suburbs.

TIP

Sometimes one event can trigger a reaction that has far-reaching results. This process is called *cause and effect*. The effect is the thing that happens. The cause is the thing that makes it happen. Several effects can come from the same cause. For example, the Industrial Revolution was the cause of many effects. These effects included the growth of cities, more people working in factories, and the disappearance of farms and wilderness. As you read, try to make connections like this between causes and effects. This will help you see the "big picture" of history.

Changes in Family Life

Before the Industrial Revolution, people usually worked at home. Quite often, the whole family took part in the work. Under this system, families spent a great deal of time together in the home. It was the center of economic activity. Once the Industrial Revolution started, though, the home was no longer the economic center. Instead, the husband—and often the wife, too—worked in a factory. As more and more factories were built, more workers were needed. One way of getting these workers was to hire whole families. Husbands, wives, and children would sometimes work in the same factory.

Young women were especially affected by the Industrial Revolution. Before this period, it had been common for young women to stay at home spinning cotton and wool. With the shift from home-based industry to factory-based industry, there was no longer a need for such work. These women began to look for factory jobs. Once mothers and daughters had worked side by side at home, sharing ideas and thoughts. Now, they might work at the same factory, but at different machine-powered looms and spinners. Often, the young women had to leave home to find work.

They found work in mills that employed mainly women. Away from home for the first time in their lives, they missed their families. But, they also met women from many other regions whom they probably would not have met otherwise.

PRACTICE 45: Changes in Family Life

Circle the letter of the correct answer to each of the following questions.

1. Which of the following was NOT a change that took place during the Industrial Revolution?
   - **a.** Families worked in factories instead of at home.
   - **b.** Many young women left home for the first time to work in factories.
   - **c.** The home became the center of economic activity.
   - **d.** none of the above

2. How did the Industrial Revolution affect many young women?
   - **a.** It forced them to leave home to work in the factories.
   - **b.** They had contact with many new people.
   - **c.** They could no longer work side by side with their mothers.
   - **d.** all of the above

Social Reform

As you have learned, the Industrial Revolution led to many changes in society. Many of these changes—such as the shift to long workdays in dirty, noisy factories—took advantage of workers or other groups. In the 1800s, many people started trying to reform, or change, some of these conditions. The efforts of these groups are called **reform movements**.

One issue was that of working conditions for factory workers. In the early years of the Industrial Revolution, factory conditions were not bad in the United States. They were better than in the early English mills, where working conditions were very harsh. But, as the Industrial Revolution progressed, things began to change. As transportation improved, more and more people could sell their products in many places. This led to added competition—many businesses were trying to sell the same things to the same people. To save money and keep prices down, factory owners kept wages as low as possible and increased workers' hours. Some bosses mistreated their workers. To reform these conditions, workers tried to form unions. **Unions** are organizations of workers who join together to protect their rights. During the Industrial Revolution, most employers did not like unions. They did not want their authority threatened. Sometimes there were bloody clashes (fights) between union workers and their bosses.

Child labor was another issue that led to reform movements. Very young children were forced to work the same hours as adults, with little or no schooling. There was no required public education. Reformers thought that every child should have an education before going to work. Others thought that educated workers would be troublesome. Still others did not want to pay for public schools. However, the idea began to spread. In 1821, the first public high school was opened in Boston, Massachusetts.

Many reform movements focused on more than one cause. Some groups called for women's rights as well as for an end to slavery. The first women's rights convention was held in July 1848, in Seneca Falls, New York. It issued a statement that sounded much like the Declaration of Independence, with one important difference: "We hold these truths to be self-evident: that all men *and women* are created equal. . . ."

PRACTICE 46: Social Reform

Check each statement below that is TRUE.

☐ **1.** Reform movements are efforts to reform, or change, conditions in society.

☐ **2.** Factory working conditions in the United States were harsh.

☐ **3.** Most employers supported workers' attempts to improve their working conditions.

☐ **4.** Many reformers wanted children to be educated before they had to start working.

☐ **5.** Some reform movements focused on more than one issue, such as women's rights and an end to slavery.

THINK ABOUT IT

Before the Industrial Revolution, skills were often passed from parent to child. Farmers taught their children the same methods they had used. Craftspeople taught their children a special skill, again using the methods and tools they used themselves. How might this have changed during and after the Industrial Revolution? Why? Write your answer on a separate sheet of paper.

A Period of Change

You have learned about the dark side of the Industrial Revolution. Yet, it also brought some positive changes, such as being able to buy more goods cheaply. It provided jobs for men and women. It made farming more efficient. Roads were built and improved. Railroads connected distant places, carrying goods and passengers.

All in all, the Industrial Revolution was a period of dramatic change. It was a time of new inventions and ideas, many of which continue to affect the United States today.

PRACTICE 47: A Period of Change

Circle the letter of the correct answer to each of the following questions.

1. Which of the following was NOT a change that happened during the Industrial Revolution?
- **a.** More goods were available at cheaper prices.
- **b.** More jobs were provided for both men and women.
- **c.** Farming became more efficient.
- **d.** Fewer people worked in the cities and more worked at home.

2. Which statement about the Industrial Revolution is TRUE?
- **a.** Its effects were only temporary; they did not last long.
- **b.** It had only negative effects.
- **c.** It had only positive effects.
- **d.** Many developments of this period continue to affect life today.

LESSON 8: Immigration

GOAL: To identify the trends, effects, and issues related to immigration in the late nineteenth and early twentieth centuries

WORDS TO KNOW

Chinese Exclusion Act	**naturalization**
emigrated	**oath**
ethnic group	**open immigration policy**
famine	**prejudice**
foreigners	**quotas**
immigrants	**restrictions**
Know-Nothing Party	**waves of immigration**

From Foreign Shores

Foreigners are people who come from outside a country. Foreigners may come to a country just to visit. Other foreigners move to a country to live. People who move to another country are called **immigrants**.

All through its history, the United States has drawn immigrants to its shores. The very first colonists were immigrants. Over the years, waves of people have come from different parts of the world. During and after the Industrial Revolution, many people in other countries heard about the growth of industry in the United States. They thought they would have a better chance of making a living in America. As a result, more people came to this country than ever before, mostly from Europe. They **emigrated**, or left their homelands, mainly to find work. They thought of America as the land of opportunity where they might have a chance at a good life.

Most immigrants who came after the Industrial Revolution settled in areas where they could find jobs most easily. These places were mostly the urban centers, or big cities, of the North. However, there were also many farmers looking for cheap land.

The flow of immigrants and the growth of cities accelerated (got faster) in the middle of the nineteenth century. In the mid-1800s, the largest groups came from Ireland and Germany. In Ireland, a disease had wiped out one of the country's most important crops—potatoes—from 1845 to 1847. This created a famine. A **famine** is a shortage of food. Many Irish people emigrated to escape the famine in their native country. In Germany, political unrest led many people to leave. They came to the United States in search of better lives.

Immigrants tend to settle in places where others from their native country already live. In the 1800s, most Irish immigrants headed mostly for New York City, Boston, and other cities in the Northeast. German immigrants settled on farms or in the large cities of the Midwest.

PRACTICE 48: From Foreign Shores

Check each statement below that is TRUE.

- ☐ **1.** Even the earliest colonists of the United States were immigrants.
- ☐ **2.** Few immigrants came to the United States during the Industrial Revolution because they did not want factory jobs.
- ☐ **3.** Immigrants expected a better life in the United States than they had in their native countries.
- ☐ **4.** Many Irish immigrants came to the United States to escape a potato famine.
- ☐ **5.** Immigrants tend to settle where other people from their native land already live.
- ☐ **6.** German immigrants mostly settled in the Northeast.

TIP

Sometimes paragraphs are filled with information. That makes it hard to figure out the important points. When this happens, look for the paragraph's *topic sentence.* The topic sentence tells you the topic, or subject, of the paragraph. The other sentences contain details about that topic.

For example, look at the second paragraph on page 112. The first sentence is the topic sentence: "All through its history, the United States has drawn immigrants to its shores." The other sentences give details that tell *why* immigrants have come to the United States.

Waves of Immigration

Historians use the term **waves of immigration** to describe the major periods of immigration to the United States. The first wave began with the colonists of the 1600s. They came mainly from England and other European countries.

The second wave started in the 1820s and lasted until the early 1870s. This was during the Industrial Revolution. Most of these immigrants came from northern and western Europe. About one third were from Ireland. Another large group was made up of German farmers, and another of Asians (mainly Chinese). Around this time, railroad companies were looking for workers to build the new rail lines. Some workers came, worked, and went home with what they had earned. Others stayed and settled in the United States.

The third wave, from 1881 to 1920, brought more than 23 million immigrants from almost every part of the world. This wave included many more people from southern and eastern Europe than any earlier period.

Look at the chart that follows on page 115. It shows the main groups of immigrants who came to the United States between the mid-1800s and the early 1900s, and when they arrived.

Immigration to the United States, 1840s–1920s

Group	When
Irish	1840s–1850s
Germans	1840s–1880s
Asians (mainly Chinese)	1860s–1880s
Danes, Norwegians, Swedes	1870s–1900s
Poles, Jews from eastern Europe, Austrians, Czechs, Hungarians, Slovaks, Italians	1880s–1920s
Mexicans	1910–1920s

IN REAL LIFE

A fourth wave of immigration began around 1965 and is still going on today. Most of these immigrants come from Mexico, the Philippines, China, Taiwan, and Cuba. Many are settling in California, New York, and Florida.

PRACTICE 49: Waves of Immigration

Circle the letter of the correct answer to each of the following questions.

1. When was the first wave of immigration?
- **a.** the 1600s
- **b.** the 1820s to the 1870s
- **c.** 1881 to the 1920s
- **d.** 1965 to the present

2. When was the second wave of immigration?
- **a.** the 1600s
- **b.** the 1820s to the 1870s
- **c.** 1881 to the 1920s
- **d.** 1965 to the present

3. When was the third wave of immigration?
   a. the 1600s
   b. the 1820s to the 1870s
   c. 1881 to the 1920s
   d. 1965 to the present

4. Which wave of immigration included the most people from southern and eastern Europe?
   a. the first wave
   b. the second wave
   c. the third wave
   d. none of the above

IMMIGRANT PORTRAIT

The Statue of Liberty (1884–)

Sculptor: Frédéric-Auguste Bartholdi
Native country: France

Most immigrants who traveled to the United States in the late 1800s and early 1900s came by ship. As they approached the shores of the United States, one of the first things they saw was the Statue of Liberty. You might say that the Statue of Liberty was also an immigrant. The statue was a gift from France to the United States. France raised $400,000 for the 151-foot statue. Americans raised $270,000 for the 89-foot pedestal on which "Lady Liberty" stands. It took 214 crates to ship the statue across the Atlantic Ocean in pieces. The statue stands on Liberty Island, not far from Ellis Island, in New York Harbor. Ellis Island is where many immigrants first set foot on American soil.

Anti-Immigrant Feelings

The waves of people coming to the United States in the 1800s contributed to some of the problems you have already learned about. One problem was overcrowding in the cities. Another issue was prejudice. **Prejudice** is the feeling that certain groups of people are different from other people in a negative way. Prejudice is not based on facts. Instead, it is usually the result of fear or ignorance. In the 1800s, many Americans were prejudiced against the new immigrants.

One reason for this prejudice was a belief that the new immigrants were taking jobs away from native-born Americans. It was true that most immigrants were used to working for less money than workers who had been in the United States for some time. Factory owners could get away with paying these immigrant workers lower wages. As a result, many higher-paid workers lost their jobs to people willing to work for less pay. The immigrants had little choice but to take the low-paying jobs if they were to survive. Often, they took the jobs that were the hardest and the dirtiest.

A second reason for prejudice against immigrants was that they were clannish. That is, they stuck together. People who come from the same country and share such things as culture and religion are called an **ethnic group**. People from the same ethnic group often lived close to one another. For example, one city might have separate Italian, Irish, Chinese, and Jewish neighborhoods. In these neighborhoods, signs were often written in the original language of the people who lived there. That language was spoken on the street and in the stores, along with English. This tendency for ethnic groups to cluster together into distinct neighborhoods kept them separate from other Americans. For many native-born Americans, this increased their feeling that the new immigrants were "different" from them.

In 1854, some native-born Americans formed a party based on their prejudice against foreigners. They were called the **Know-Nothing Party**. If anyone asked them about their group, they answered, "I know nothing." Many of the party's members were workers who had had to compete for jobs with freed blacks and immigrants. In New England, the Know-Nothings opposed the Irish immigrants. In California, the Know-Nothings opposed Chinese immigrants who worked on the new western railroad lines. Members of the Know-Nothing Party ran for state offices in some states. Some even won their races. In 1856, the Know-Nothing Party nominated former U.S. president Millard Fillmore as their candidate for president. However, Fillmore won only one state. The Know-Nothing Party soon disappeared.

Millard Fillmore

TIP

One way to better understand events and trends in history is to compare them with similar events and trends today. As you have read, a fourth wave of immigration to the United States is going on today. You may be familiar with some anti-immigration sentiment. How does this wave compare with those of the 1800s and early 1900s? In 2005, 11 percent of the U.S. population was foreign-born. This means that about 11 out of every 100 people in the United States were born outside the country. This may seem like a large amount. However, in 1910, almost 15 percent of the U.S. population was foreign-born—more than today! This may help you understand how large the second and third waves of immigration were, and how they affected the rest of society.

PRACTICE 50: Anti-Immigrant Feelings

Decide if each statement below is true (**T**) or false (**F**). Write the letter of the correct answer on the line before each statement.

____ **1.** Prejudice is a love for all people, regardless of their backgrounds or lifestyles.

____ **2.** New immigrants took jobs for low pay because they wanted to take the jobs of native-born Americans.

____ **3.** People from the same ethnic group tended to live close to one another.

____ **4.** The Know-Nothing Party was based on prejudice against foreigners.

IMMIGRANT PORTRAIT

Jacob August Riis (1849–1914)

Newspaper writer, reformer
Native country: Denmark

Jacob Riis was a Danish immigrant. He was shocked by the poor living conditions of other immigrants in New York City. He wrote a book about it in 1890 called *How the Other Half Lives.* In large part because of this book, living conditions improved for many people. Riis wrote several other books about the lives of the urban poor. He also established the Jacob A. Riis Neighborhood Settlement House for social work.

Limits on Immigration

The Civil War started in 1861. Before then, about 400,000 new immigrants arrived in the United States in any given year. By the time the war ended in 1865, this number was closer to 750,000 per year. At this time, the United States had an **open immigration policy**. This meant that there was no limit on the number of new immigrants who could enter the country each year.

As the numbers of new immigrants increased, people began wondering whether American society could absorb all of them. They wondered if there would be enough housing and jobs for everyone. Some feared that the newcomers would soon outnumber native-born Americans. In some cities, as much as half of the population was made up of either immigrants or the children of immigrants.

By 1865, some native-born Americans were demanding that limits be set on the number of immigrants allowed into the country. Calls for such **quotas**, or limits, on immigration got loudest when there were economic problems and people lost jobs. The people who called for quotas tended to focus their demands on certain countries. In 1882, for example, Congress passed a law called the **Chinese Exclusion Act**. This act banned entry to most people from China. No new Chinese immigrants would be allowed into the United States for ten years. The Chinese Exclusion Act was extended (continued) several times. It did not end until 1943.

Even now, the United States does not have a totally open immigration policy. There are **restrictions**, or limits, on who can enter the country. Also, only certain numbers and certain types of people can become American citizens. For example, criminals or people connected to terrorist groups are not allowed. There are quotas on the number of people who are allowed to immigrate each year. For example, there might be a quota of 500,000. If a person who wants to enter is number 500,001, he or she would not be allowed to immigrate that year.

THINK ABOUT IT

At one time, the United States had a higher quota for immigrants from Europe than from Asia and Africa. This meant that more people from Europe could come to the United States than from Asia or Africa. Why do you think this was so? Do you think this policy was fair? Write your answer on a separate sheet of paper.

PRACTICE 51: Limits on Immigration

Check each statement below that is TRUE.

☐ **1.** Before the Civil War, there was no limit on immigration to the United States.

☐ **2.** After the Civil War, the number of immigrants started to decrease.

☐ **3.** After the Civil War, people started demanding limits on the number of immigrants allowed in the country each year.

☐ **4.** Calls for quotas, or limits, on immigration were strongest during times of strong economic growth.

☐ **5.** Today, the United States has a completely open immigration policy.

THINK ABOUT IT

Perhaps some of your family immigrated to the United States during the 1800s or later. How would your life be different if quotas had kept your family members from coming to America? How do you feel about setting quotas for today's wave of immigration? Write your answer on a separate sheet of paper.

Naturalization

To become citizens of the United States, immigrants must meet certain requirements. First, they must have been a resident of the United States for five years. After five years, they can file a form with the government. With this form, they request, or ask for, citizenship. The government then checks to make sure that the applicants are of good character. The applicants must also pass a test in English, American government, and American history. When applications are approved, a court gives the applicants an oath. An **oath** is a type of promise. In this case, it is a promise of loyalty to the United States. This series of steps is called the process of **naturalization**.

A naturalized citizen can do almost anything a native-born citizen can do. There is only one restriction. Currently, a naturalized citizen cannot become president of the United States. This restriction goes back to the time when the U.S. Constitution was written. The Founding Fathers were afraid of foreign influence. They were afraid that someone might become president who was loyal to another country.

PRACTICE 52: Naturalization

Circle the letter of the correct answer to each of the following questions.

1. What is the naturalization process?

- **a.** the process of setting quotas on immigration
- **b.** the process of immigrating to the United States
- **c.** the process of becoming a U.S. citizen
- **d.** the process of leaving one land to live in another

2. What does an immigrant have to do to become a naturalized U.S. citizen?
   a. live in the United States for at least five years
   b. file a special form with the government
   c. pass a test in English, American government, and American history
   d. all of the above

3. What must an applicant for naturalization promise?
   a. to obey the law
   b. to be loyal to the United States
   c. to run for political office
   d. to speak only English

4. What is the one thing a naturalized citizen cannot do?
   a. vote
   b. get a job
   c. pay taxes
   d. become president of the United States

IMMIGRANT PORTRAIT

Andrew Carnegie (1835–1919)

Industrialist, philanthropist
Native country: Scotland

Andrew Carnegie was an immigrant from Scotland who made a fortune in the U.S. steel industry. He ended up as one of the world's richest men. Carnegie gave away most of his money to support such causes as world peace, education, and medical research. Carnegie once said that any man who dies rich, dies disgraced. By the time he died, this naturalized American had given away more than 350 million dollars.

LESSON 9: Isolationism Versus Internationalism

GOAL: To identify the shifts between isolationism and internationalism in American history

WORDS TO KNOW

alliance	**isolationist**	**prosperity**
authorized	**League of Nations**	**Treaty of Versailles**
Great Depression	**neutrality**	**United Nations**
internationalism	**propaganda**	

Early Neutrality

As you learned in Lesson 1, the way a nation deals with other nations is called its foreign policy. Foreign policy differs from country to country. Some nations prefer to keep to themselves. Others get more involved in world affairs. One country's foreign policy can also change as the world situation changes. Today, for example, the United States is involved with other nations in many different ways. Throughout most of its history, though, the United States tried to stay out of the affairs of other nations.

Before the Revolutionary War, England decided the foreign policy of its American colonies. Naturally, England's decisions were based on its own interests, not those of the colonies. During the Revolutionary War, the colonies took advantage of some of Europe's old quarrels. The French and the English had been enemies for centuries. So, the colonies asked for France's help in defeating the English. In fact, France's help was key to the American victory.

The alliance with France, though, was a temporary one. An **alliance** is an agreement between nations. Nations form alliances because they have common, or like, interests. For example, if several countries are afraid of one particular country, they might form a military alliance. The alliance means that if one member is attacked, the others will come to its aid. The alliance between the American colonies and France lasted only for the length of the war. After the war was over and the colonies were independent, they shifted their foreign policy.

Once the United States became independent, it could form its own foreign policy. For example, the United States needed to develop its economy. It wanted to trade with other countries. But, it did not want to become involved in Europe's political problems. Instead, the United States followed a policy of **neutrality**. This means that it did not take sides in disagreements among European nations. It also avoided permanent (long-lasting) alliances.

It was President George Washington who first stated this policy of neutrality as his term in office ended. It is not hard to understand why he did so. At the time, Europe seemed always to be involved in a war. Sometimes, European nations were fighting people in countries they had colonized. This was what England did with the United States during the Revolutionary War. At other times, European nations fought one another.

Washington urged future American governments to do more business with other nations. However, he also advised them to limit their political connections. Washington believed that Europe and the United States did not have the same interests. Getting involved in Europe's problems would only endanger the peace and prosperity of the United States. (**Prosperity** is a time when the economy is doing well.)

■ PRACTICE 53: Early Neutrality

Check each statement below that is TRUE.

- ☐ **1.** Foreign policy is the way in which a government deals with other countries.
- ☐ **2.** An alliance is an agreement between nations.
- ☐ **3.** The United States has never had an alliance with another country.
- ☐ **4.** Neutrality means not taking sides.
- ☐ **5.** George Washington urged future governments not to conduct trade with other nations.
- ☐ **6.** The United States could take sides in a war even with a policy of neutrality.

Isolationism

James Monroe

In 1812, the U.S. policy of neutrality was interrupted. The United States became involved in the War of 1812—even though it wanted to stay neutral. After the war, in 1823, President James Monroe made the country's neutrality clear in a document called the Monroe Doctrine. As you have learned, the Monroe Doctrine stated that America would not become involved in the affairs of Europe. It also warned Europe to stay out of American affairs.

The Monroe Doctrine told the world that the United States was taking an **isolationist** position. The term *isolated* means "separate" or "apart from others." Isolationists are interested in protecting their own nation. They want to avoid the troubles of other countries by staying out of their affairs. Another word for isolationism is *nationalism.* The opposite of nationalism and isolationism is **internationalism**. This means that a country wants to take part in world affairs. Another term for internationalism is *globalism.*

TIP

Breaking a long word apart can often help you understand its meaning. Look at the word *internationalism.* The prefix *inter-* means "between" or "among." The root word *nation* means "country." The suffix *-ism* means "a belief or system." So, the term *internationalism* means "relations between or among nations."

PRACTICE 54: Isolationism

Circle the letter of the correct answer to each of the following questions.

1. What European conflict caused the United States to break its policy of neutrality?
   a. the American Revolution
   b. the War of 1812
   c. the Civil War
   d. the French Revolution

2. Which document stated that Europe should stay out of American affairs, and that the United States would stay out of European affairs?
   a. the U.S. Constitution
   b. the Bill of Rights
   c. the Treaty of Paris
   d. the Monroe Doctrine

World War I

The neutral position stated in the Monroe Doctrine was followed by the United States for nearly 100 years. Then, in 1914, Europe exploded into World War I. The president at the time, Woodrow Wilson, issued a statement of neutrality. He insisted that the United States had neutral trading rights. That is, the United States could trade with both Germany on one side and England on the other. However, those countries did not agree with the policy. It was a dangerous situation for the United States. England controlled most shipping on the Atlantic Ocean. German submarines used torpedoes to sink merchant ships without warning.

Woodrow Wilson

In 1915, a German submarine sank an English passenger ship, the *Lusitania.* The shipwreck claimed 128 American lives. President Wilson protested strongly. For a while, Germany was more careful about what ships its submarines attacked. Nevertheless, the war dragged on and on. In 1916, the Germans told their submarine commanders to shoot at any ship headed for England. This action sent the message that the Germans no longer accepted American neutrality. Even then, Wilson was not ready to declare war. He had campaigned for reelection in 1916 with the slogan "He kept us out of war." Finally, and reluctantly, Wilson decided to act. On April 2, 1916, he asked Congress to declare war against Germany and its partners.

After almost 100 years of isolationism, Americans were not eager to fight in Europe. For one thing, many Americans (including the president and Congress) still did not trust the Europeans. Also, many Americans were of German descent. By this time, many German immigrants were living in the United States. These immigrants still felt strong ties to their native country. They did not want to go to war against Germany.

President Wilson used propaganda to convince Americans that they should get involved in this terrible war. **Propaganda** is a kind of advertising used to promote certain ideas. Wilson used such things as speeches, rallies, and movies to change American opinion. Many people remained opposed to entering the war. But, the propaganda convinced most people that the United States could not remain isolationist.

PRACTICE 55: World War I

Circle the letter of the correct answer to each of the following questions.

1. What was the position of the United States at the beginning of World War I?

- **a.** It sided with England.
- **b.** It sided with Germany.
- **c.** It did not join any side.
- **d.** It refused to trade with any country involved in the war.

2. What English ship was sunk by Germany, killing 128 Americans?

- **a.** the *Titanic*
- **b.** the *Lusitania*
- **c.** the *Queen Elizabeth II*
- **d.** the *Isolationism*

3. Why did President Wilson finally decide to declare war on Germany and its partners?

- **a.** The Germans declared that they would shoot at any ship headed for England.
- **b.** The Germans sank the *Lusitania.*
- **c.** The Germans attacked an American naval base in Hawaii.
- **d.** The Germans refused to continue trading with the United States.

4. What is propaganda?
   a. a kind of advertising used to promote certain ideas
   b. the way one country deals with other countries
   c. a policy of remaining neutral
   d. speeches that explained the causes of World War I to Americans

The League of Nations

World War I ended in 1918 with the defeat of Germany and its allies, or partners. In 1919, the winning nations drew up a peace treaty called the **Treaty of Versailles.** The treaty included a plan for an organization of nations. This organization was to be called the **League of Nations.** It was also called the Geneva League, because its headquarters was in Geneva, Switzerland. The goal of the League was to keep peace in the world.

Warren G. Harding

U.S. President Woodrow Wilson strongly supported the League of Nations. Yet many U.S. senators opposed the League. The U.S. Senate voted to reject the Versailles Treaty, and thus the League, in both 1919 and 1920. Americans showed that they approved of this decision. They elected Warren G. Harding president in 1920 partly because he opposed the League of Nations. Most Americans opposed America's entry into the League of Nations. They felt that America should return to its former policy of isolationism. They wanted the United States to devote itself to its own national interests. They thought the country should remain apart from the affairs of other nations.

Many Americans also feared that joining the League of Nations would threaten America's independence. They wanted the United States to retain, or keep, the power to make its own foreign policy decisions. If the United States joined the League, it would have to follow the policies set by the League as a whole.

When Calvin Coolidge campaigned for president in 1924, he made it clear that he felt the United States should not get involved with other countries. Coolidge easily won the election.

PRACTICE 56: The League of Nations

Decide if each statement below is true (**T**) or false (**F**). Write the letter of the correct answer on the line before each statement.

_____ **1.** The treaty that ended World War I provided a plan for the League of Nations.

_____ **2.** The goal of the League of Nations was to keep peace in the world.

_____ **3.** The United States immediately joined the League of Nations.

_____ **4.** In the beginning, most Americans wanted to join the League of Nations.

_____ **5.** Most Americans wanted the United States to return to isolationism.

_____ **6.** If the United States joined the League of Nations, it would have to follow the foreign policy set by the League as a whole.

THINK ABOUT IT

For many years, the United States kept a position of neutrality. It did not get involved with the affairs of other nations. Today, however, the United States is not neutral. It gets involved in the economic and political affairs of several nations. What do you think is best for the country—neutrality or involvement in world affairs? Why? Write your answer on a separate sheet of paper.

World War II

After World War I, America followed its isolationist policies. It worked for its own economic development. Then, in 1929, the United States and most other countries were hit by the **Great Depression**. This was a deep, worldwide economic slowdown. Millions of people lost their jobs. Even those who had work were paid less. In the United States, President Franklin Roosevelt concentrated on saving the economy and putting people back to work.

While the United States was focusing on problems at home, Germany was on the move again. It had been busily preparing for war. In fact, it was equipped for war as no nation had ever been. Germany started taking over other countries one by one. World War II was soon underway. In Asia, Japan was doing the same thing. The two nations formed a military alliance, along with Italy. It seemed as though Germany and Japan wanted to take over the world and divide it between them.

Again, America tried to remain neutral. It did, however, try to help the countries that were at war with Germany, especially England. It was not easy to convince the American people and Congress that it was right to get involved. Roosevelt's argument was that, with America's help, England and its allies would win the war. Then the United States would never have to fight. Roosevelt explained that it was important to strengthen the countries under attack. The United States sent ships, planes, guns, and ammunition to England and the Soviet Union, among others.

THINK ABOUT IT

The Lend-Lease Act of 1941 let the United States give military aid to the nations then involved in World War II. The act **authorized**, or allowed, the president to send arms or other materials to "the government of any country whose defense the President deems vital to the defense of the United States." The words *deems vital* are key. If President Roosevelt deemed, or felt, that it was vital (necessary), he could act. Under that act, the United States helped England, the Soviet Union, China, and many other countries.

Not everyone in Congress voted for the Lend-Lease Act. One of the leading isolationists was Senator Robert Taft. (He was the son of William Howard Taft, the twenty-seventh president.) He pointed out that the bill would "give the President power to carry on a kind of undeclared war all over the world, in which America would do everything except actually put soldiers in the front-line trenches where the fighting is."

If you had been in Congress at the time, would you have voted for the Lend-Lease Act? Explain your reasons. Write your answer on a separate sheet of paper.

Because of its isolationist policies, the United States was not prepared for war. So, it began to build up its armed forces. It normally takes several years to prepare for war. This is what the United States did as the war raged in Europe and Asia. Meanwhile, the country's official policy was still neutrality.

However, on December 7, 1941, Japan attacked Pearl Harbor. Pearl Harbor is an American military base in Hawaii. At the time, America was actually trying to arrange a treaty with Japan. Once Pearl Harbor was attacked, though, the United States could no longer stay out of the war. Suddenly, America was at war on two fronts: Europe and Asia. Its isolationist policy was interrupted once more.

PRACTICE 57: World War II

Circle the letter of the correct answer to each of the following questions.

1. Why did President Roosevelt want to help the countries at war in Europe?

- **a.** He thought it would help England win the war sooner, so the United States would not have to fight.
- **b.** He secretly wanted the United States to go to war again.
- **c.** Germany had declared war on the United States.
- **d.** He wanted to help Germany and Japan win the war quickly.

2. Why was the United States not prepared for war?

- **a.** because of the Great Depression
- **b.** because many Americans had been out of work
- **c.** because it had been following a policy of isolationism
- **d.** because it wanted to keep its weapons secret

3. What official policy did the United States follow while it prepared for war?

- **a.** It sided with England and its allies.
- **b.** It sided with Germany and Japan.
- **c.** It kept a position of neutrality.
- **d.** It refused to help any country that was at war.

4. What military action drew the United States into World War II?
   a. Germany's invasion of Poland
   b. the sinking of the *Lusitania*
   c. Japan's attack on Pearl Harbor
   d. the passing of the Lend-Lease Act

From Isolationism to Internationalism

By 1945, Germany, Japan, and their partners had been defeated by the United States, England, and their partners. The United States came out of World War II as the most powerful nation in the world. The push to arm the country and prepare for war had helped rebuild American industry. American successes in the war had restored the nation's confidence. The Great Depression was a thing of the past. Now, the United States realized that, with its size and wealth, it could no longer remain apart from world affairs. The United States had taken a leading role in World War II. Its entrance into the war had made the difference between success and defeat for England and its allies. After the end of the war, the world looked to the United States as the leader of the democratic world.

Today, the role of the United States is far from isolationist. For example, the United States is now a member of the **United Nations**. This international organization was set up in 1945 to "establish and maintain a just and lasting peace." The United States has formed a number of military alliances to protect itself and other nations from threats of war. It also gives economic aid to nations around the world.

The switch from isolationism to internationalism did not take place overnight. Even today, isolationist attitudes have not completely disappeared. You may have heard protests against the role of the United States in the United Nations. And, in 2001, the United States dropped out of an international agreement about taking steps to reduce global warming. People still voice concerns about giving up national independence to international organizations and alliances. But, it is not likely that the United States will ever be as isolationist as it once was. The country has found that its own interests call for close ties with other countries.

PRACTICE 58: From Isolationism to Internationalism

Check each statement below that is TRUE.

☐ **1.** After World War II, the United States was the most powerful nation in the world.

☐ **2.** After World War II, the United States went back to isolationism.

☐ **3.** The United States joined the United Nations.

☐ **4.** Since World War II, the United States has refused to form any military alliances with other nations.

☐ **5.** Some people still worry about the United States giving up national independence to international organizations.

☐ **6.** The entry of the United States into World War II had little effect on the outcome of the war.

☐ **7.** The United States has always refused to give economic aid to other countries.

IN REAL LIFE

After World War II, U.S. foreign policy changed forever. One of the most important changes was the desire to keep peace throughout the world. One example of this foreign policy is an organization called the Peace Corps. The Peace Corps was started by President John F. Kennedy in 1961. It was founded to encourage the growth and improvement of other countries. Skilled Peace Corps volunteers travel to countries around the world to share their knowledge. They help in the areas of education, agriculture, health, trade, technology, crafts, and community development. Today, Peace Corps volunteers still offer assistance to other countries. They work especially with people who have suffered the effects of war or poverty.

UNIT 3 REVIEW

Circle the letter of the correct answer to each of the following questions.

1. What are interchangeable parts?
   a. engines powered by steam
   b. pieces of machines that are not necessary
   c. parts that are made the same way every time
   d. wooden gun parts

2. What was one result of the Industrial Revolution?
   a. Families started working in factories instead of at home.
   b. More and more young women worked at home with their mothers.
   c. More and more people lived on small farms.
   d. Families started spending more time together at home.

3. What was one result of reformers calling attention to child labor?
   a. the convention in Seneca Falls, New York
   b. the abolition of slavery
   c. more opportunities for women
   d. calls for public education

4. Why did most immigrants settle in urban centers?
   a. because they did not like farm life
   b. because that was where the jobs were
   c. because they could not afford houses in the country
   d. all of the above

5. What was one reason for anti-immigrant feelings in the 1800s?
   a. competition for jobs
   b. the spread of famine to the United States
   c. lack of farmland
   d. immigrants getting better pay than native-born Americans

6. What was the purpose of setting quotas on immigration?
   a. to encourage more foreigners to come to the United States each year
   b. to limit immigration from China
   c. to limit the number of children immigrants could have
   d. to limit the number of immigrants allowed into the United States each year

7. In 1914, what did President Woodrow Wilson want the United States to do?
   a. trade with both Germany and England
   b. control shipping on the Atlantic Ocean
   c. destroy German submarines
   d. help England and not Germany

8. When did President Wilson ask Congress to declare war?
   a. when American lives were lost on the *Lusitania*
   b. when he had to run for reelection
   c. when the Germans no longer accepted American neutrality
   d. when propaganda did not work

9. Why did most Americans NOT want the United States to join the League of Nations?
   a. They feared the United States would lose some of its independence.
   b. They wanted to return to isolationism.
   c. They wanted the United States to continue making its own foreign policy.
   d. all of the above

10. What event drew the United States into World War II?
   a. a treaty with Japan
   b. the alliance of Japan, Germany, and Italy
   c. Japan's attack on Pearl Harbor
   d. the desire to help England

UNIT 3 APPLICATION ACTIVITY 1

Shared Traditions

Look at the two circles below. You will use these circles to make a Venn diagram. This type of diagram is an easy way to show the similarities and differences between two things. In this case, it will be two people. (You may wish to copy the diagram on another sheet of paper.)

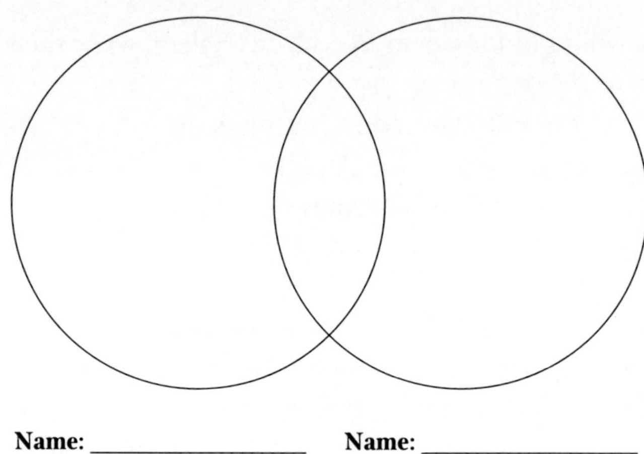

Name: ___________________ **Name:** ___________________

First, choose a partner. You can choose another learner in your class, a friend, or a neighbor. If possible, choose someone whose background is somewhat different from your own. Then, label each circle above with one of your names.

Now, find a quiet spot to talk with your partner. Discuss the different traditions each of you follow. Here are some questions you may want to ask each other:

- How do you celebrate your birthday?
- What do you do for entertainment?
- What holidays do you observe?
- What do you do for chores?
- What kind of meals do you eat?

As you talk with your partner, take notes in the Venn diagram. When something your partner does is similar to something you do, write it in the space where the circles overlap. When something your partner does is different from what you do, write what your partner does in his or her circle. Then, write what you do in your own circle. When you finish, the Venn diagram will show which traditions you and your partner share and which are different.

UNIT 3 APPLICATION ACTIVITY 2

Inventive Minds

Below is a chart that lists the names of some inventors whose work has changed the world. Use encyclopedias and/or the Internet to complete the chart. Find out what each person invented, when the invention(s) was (or were) developed, and how the invention(s) changed people's lives.

Name of Inventor	Invention and Date	How It Changed the World
Alexander Graham Bell		
Henry Bessemer		
Johannes Gutenberg		
Levi Strauss		
Josephine Cochran		

UNIT 3 APPLICATION ACTIVITY 3

Ethnic Foods

One of the customs that immigrants take to another country is the way they prepare food. Cities of all sizes usually have what are called "ethnic" restaurants. These eating places serve foods that originally came from countries all around the world.

Using the Yellow Pages of your local telephone book, look under *Restaurants.* On the lines below, list the different types of restaurants in your town or city, such as Thai, Chinese, Italian, Mexican, and so forth.

______________________________ ______________________________

______________________________ ______________________________

______________________________ ______________________________

______________________________ ______________________________

______________________________ ______________________________

Now, find a small map of the world and make a copy of it. On the map, locate the country from which each type of food you listed comes. Mark each of these countries on the map with an *X*. Finally, study your marked-up map. Do the ethnic restaurants in your town represent many countries? Are most of the foods from a specific region?

On the lines below, write a few sentences describing your marked-up map. What does the map tell you about your town?

____

____

____

____

____

____

____

UNIT 4
Twentieth-Century America and Beyond

LESSON 10: America from 1900 to 1930

GOAL: To demonstrate knowledge of the events, people, and trends of American history from 1900 to 1930

WORDS TO KNOW

Allies	**middle class**
American Federation of Labor (AFL)	**platform**
arbitration	**Populist Party**
Black Tuesday	**Progressive movement**
Central Powers	**Prohibition**
collective bargaining	**Roaring Twenties**
corporations	**Sherman Antitrust Act**
dollar diplomacy	**speakeasies**
Federal Trade Commission (FTC)	**stocks**
imperialism	**strike**
investors	**temperance movement**
Jazz Age	**trust**
majority	**women's suffrage movement**

The Populist Revolt

The United States grew at an amazing rate during the 1800s. Would the country experience similar growth during the 1900s? This lesson will explore American history in the first decades of the twentieth century, from 1900 to 1930.

After the U.S. Civil War ended in 1865, American industry boomed. Large **corporations**—businesses owned by many stockholders—gained power and control. By the end of the nineteenth century, a group of about

4,000 millionaires controlled American industry. They also controlled much of the government. One third of the seats in the Senate were held by millionaires. They decided who would be nominated for president. They were not interested in passing laws that might improve the lives of people less fortunate than themselves.

Many people united against these millionaires under the banner of the **Populist Party**. The members of this party included farmers, cattle ranchers, miners, and small-town businesspeople. The Populist **platform**, or statement of goals, of 1892 called for the following:

- public ownership of the railroads, and telephone, telegraph, and postal systems
- creation of an income tax that would make the wealthy pay more and equalize (even out) wealth
- popular election of senators

The Populist ticket won more than a million votes in the 1892 presidential election. But, the Democratic candidate, Grover Cleveland, still won. Then, in 1893, the country fell into an economic depression. About 500 banks closed down. Close to 3 million people were unemployed. President Cleveland was blamed for the country's problems.

Grover Cleveland

At the Democratic convention in 1896, the Democratic party endorsed many Populist goals. These included a lower tariff, an income tax, and less power for large corporations. Cleveland lost the nomination to William Jennings Bryan, a powerful speaker who won the support of the Populists. However, many wealthy people gave money to the campaign of the Republican candidate, Senator William McKinley. His campaign raised ten times as much money as Bryan's. In the election, McKinley defeated Bryan. The Populist movement died out after McKinley became president. The economy improved, and the goals of the Populists were no longer urgent.

William McKinley

■ PRACTICE 59: The Populist Revolt

Decide if each statement below is true (T) or false (F). Write the correct letter on the line before each statement.

_____ **1.** The Populist Party was opposed to the powerful corporations.

_____ **2.** William Jennings Bryan won the election of 1896.

The Search for Empire

The United States did not want to become involved in the affairs of other countries. Yet, that did not stop the government from taking territory around the world. This is known as **imperialism**, or the building of an empire. The United States, like other nations, was looking for raw materials for its factories and markets for its finished products.

Hawaii was one of the first places to fall to American imperialism. In 1893, a handful of Americans living in Hawaii began a revolt. The United States sent 150 marines there to overthrow the government of Queen Liliuokalani. Hawaii became a territory of the United States in 1900. In 1959, it became the country's fiftieth state.

THINK ABOUT IT

Imagine the year is 1893. You are a native of Hawaii. A group of Americans has just overthrown your queen and formed a new government. How do you feel about these changes? What could be some advantages of becoming part of the United States? What are the disadvantages? Write your answer on a separate sheet of paper.

President McKinley strongly supported imperialism. The Spanish empire in the Pacific and Caribbean was crumbling. The United States was eyeing Cuba, an island in the Caribbean Sea just south of Florida. The United States wanted to benefit from Cuba's resources—its sugar plantations and cheap labor. Cubans were unhappy with Spanish rule. They were especially bothered by the cruel policies imposed by General Valeriano Weyler.

In 1898, anti-Spanish riots broke out in Havana, the capital of Cuba. President McKinley ordered the U.S.S. *Maine* to sail to Cuba to protect Americans living there. On February 15, 1898, an explosion sank the *Maine,* killing 260 sailors. No one could prove that Spain was responsible for the explosion. However, ill feeling toward Spain ran high. Newspaper headlines such as "Remember the *Maine*! To hell with Spain!" stirred up the public.

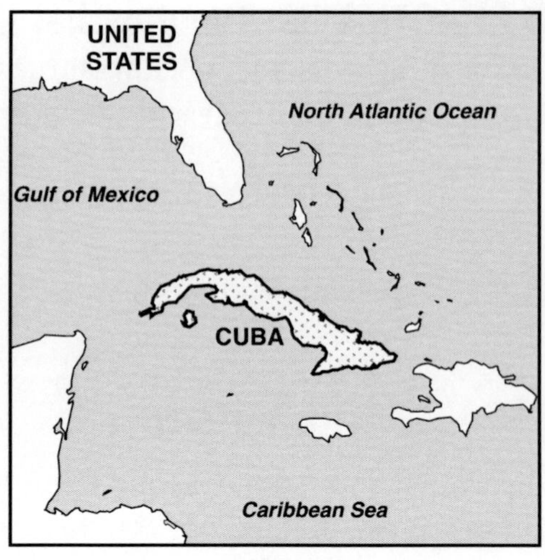

Cuba

Spain finally declared war on the United States on April 24, 1898. The United States responded by declaring war on Spain the next day. The war, called the Spanish-American War, was quickly won by the United States. In December 1898, Spain accepted defeat in a new Treaty of Paris. Cuba became an independent country. The territories of Guam, Puerto Rico, and the Philippines came under American control. The American empire was underway.

PRACTICE 60: The Search for Empire

Circle the letter of the correct answer to each of the following questions.

1. What term means the taking of territories around the world?
- **a.** territorialism
- **b.** imperialism
- **c.** fanaticism
- **d.** foreign policy

2. Where did the Spanish-American War begin?
- **a.** Havana
- **b.** Washington, D.C.
- **c.** Manila Harbor
- **d.** Madrid

Dollar Diplomacy in Latin America

President McKinley was assassinated in 1901. After the assassination, Vice President Theodore Roosevelt became president. Like McKinley, Roosevelt favored American imperialism. With the motto "Speak softly and carry a big stick," he quickly built up American naval power. As American businesses increased their international trading, there was a need to protect their interests. Roosevelt sent the navy around the world to support American interests.

Theodore Roosevelt

Roosevelt declared that it was up to the United States to act when there was continued "wrongdoing" in Latin America. He claimed an "international police power" for the United States in the region. Roosevelt immediately applied this doctrine in the Dominican Republic, an island nation just east of Haiti. The Dominican Republic was in debt to several European countries. It also owed money to American **investors**—people who invest, or put money into, businesses. In 1905, President Roosevelt gave an executive order taking charge of the Dominican Republic's finances.

In 1909, William H. Taft became the next president. Like Roosevelt, Taft believed in American investment in other countries, especially in Latin America. Under Taft's administration, a foreign policy called "dollar diplomacy" began. **Dollar diplomacy** means lending other countries money, then using their debts to influence affairs in those countries. Suppose the U.S. government felt that American investments in a country were threatened. Using dollar diplomacy, it could interfere in that country's affairs to protect the investments. The Taft administration tried to use dollar diplomacy in Nicaragua and then China. Neither attempt was successful, however. The administration abandoned the policy in 1912.

William H. Taft

Yet, the United States continued to interfere with Latin America. For example, the U.S. Navy seized Vera Cruz in Mexico in 1914. Also that year, U.S. Marines went into Haiti and the Dominican Republic.

■ PRACTICE 61: Dollar Diplomacy in Latin America

Decide if each statement below is true (**T**) or false (**F**). Write the correct letter on the line before each statement.

_____ **1.** President Taft said, "Speak softly and carry a big stick."

_____ **2.** *Dollar diplomacy* is a term that describes a policy protecting U.S. investments in foreign countries.

_____ **3.** Dollar diplomacy was used to justify U.S. involvement in Latin-American affairs.

The Progressive Movement and Organized Labor

Back in the United States, wealthy people benefited from the booming economy. Many others, however, did not enjoy great wealth or power. These people, called the **middle class,** joined with the working class populists to form the **Progressive movement.** This movement lasted from about 1890 until 1917. Its aim was to change America's economic and political practices.

The Progressives wanted these reforms:

- more direct democracy by having the public vote on laws
- conservation of natural resources
- women's suffrage (voting rights)
- the prohibition of (a ban on) alcohol
- an inheritance tax
- safety laws to protect workers
- restrictions on child labor

Democrats and Republicans alike joined the Progressive movement. The Progressives were concerned with problems related to city life. They worked to pass laws banning unsafe working and housing conditions. President Theodore Roosevelt was responsible for many reforms. He demanded that "big business give the people a square deal." One of Roosevelt's goals was to break up the huge trusts that controlled so much of American business. A **trust** is a group of large companies that agree to work together. They do this so that they have less competition. Small companies are threatened and can be put out of business by a trust. The **Sherman Antitrust Act** of 1890 made it illegal for anyone to form a trust. Roosevelt also pushed through laws that protected natural resources, such as land and water. He also worked for laws on food, drugs, and railroad rates.

Meanwhile, American workers were organizing themselves to improve wages and working conditions. The **American Federation of Labor (AFL)** was established in 1890. It was the country's largest labor union. Members included skilled workers, such as printers, brewers, and carpenters. Union members hoped to reach their goals by **collective bargaining** (discussions with management). If they could not resolve their issues with management, they were willing to strike. A **strike** happens when workers refuse to go to work until their demands are met by management.

Organized labor took on big business in May 1902. Nearly 150,000 men of the AFL's United Mine Workers walked out of the mines in eastern Pennsylvania. The nation was faced with a coal shortage as winter approached. President Roosevelt stepped in. He threatened to take over the mines in order to bring the workers and management to an agreement. The mine operators finally accepted arbitration. In **arbitration**, both sides agree to follow the ruling of a third party. That person, the arbitrator, has no loyalties to either side. The arbitrator for this dispute cut the workers' hours and gave them a 10 percent increase in wages.

Roosevelt's action was unusual. Until then, the government had followed a hands-off approach toward big business. When Roosevelt was elected president in 1904, he continued to battle big business.

TIP

Taking notes in the form of an outline can help you keep track of important ideas, people, and dates. Here is one way you might outline the last two pages:

I. The Progressive Movement

- A. Banned unsafe working and housing conditions
- B. Eliminated large trusts
  - a. broke up monopolies
  - b. increased competition
  - c. kept small companies in business
  - d. Sherman Antitrust Act of 1890

II. American workers organized

- A. Workers wanted to improve wages and dangerous conditions
- B. Workers held collective bargaining—discussions with management
- C. Workers were willing to strike
  - a. AFL's United Mine Workers had strike
  - b. nation faced with coal shortage
  - c. Roosevelt threatened to take over mines
  - d. mine operators accepted arbitration

You might organize this information differently. Use the system that works best for you.

■ PRACTICE 62: The Progressive Movement and Organized Labor

Circle the letter of the correct answer to each of the following questions.

1. What is a group of companies that agree to work together?
 a. a union
 b. a trust
 c. a stock exchange
 d. a monopoly

2. What is it called when two sides agree to follow the rules of a third party?
 a. arbitration
 b. a strike
 c. negotiation
 d. giving in

Woodrow Wilson and World War I

In 1912, Woodrow Wilson was the Democratic candidate for president. He called for more antitrust laws and reform of the nation's banking system. He won. The Democrats also won a majority in Congress. A **majority** is more than half of any group (in this case, the members of Congress). The Democrats could get bills they wanted through Congress easily. These included a personal income tax, a banking reform bill, and the establishment of the **Federal Trade Commission (FTC)**. The FTC's responsibility is to prevent one company from destroying another by unfai

Woodrow Wilson

Unlike earlier presidents, Wilson was against imperialism. He did not want to get involved with foreign nations. However, in the summer of 1914, war broke out in Europe. On one side were the **Central Powers**: Austria-Hungary, Germany, and Italy. On the other side were the **Allies**: France, Great Britain, and Russia. (In 1915, Italy switched to join forces with the Allies.)

As you learned in Lesson 9, Wilson wished to remain neutral in the war. He did not want to join either the Central Powers or the Allies. In this war, new, more dangerous weapons were being used. These included using submarines, tanks, machine guns, and poison gas.

As you learned earlier, the Germans were attacking unarmed ships. In 1915, they sank the *Lusitania,* a British passenger ship. There were 1,200 passengers killed on the *Lusitania,* including 128 Americans. In 1917, the Germans told their submarine commanders to shoot at any ship headed for England. Wilson realized that the Germans no longer accepted the United States as neutral. He asked Congress to declare war against Germany and its partners. In 1917, the United States joined the Allies.

By the time the United States declared war, the Allies desperately needed weapons and manpower. Back at home, the economy of America was focused on the war effort. Both business and the government had to work together in this effort. Congress gave President Wilson control over parts of the economy. Agencies were set up to help organize war-related industries.

Together, the Americans and the Allies defeated Germany in 1918. Much of Europe lay in ruins. Eight million soldiers had died, and so had nearly as many civilians. There were 112,000 American lives lost. The victorious Allies wanted to punish Germany. They wrote up the Treaty of Versailles in 1919, which took territory away from Germany. It also forced Germany to pay 33 billion dollars to the Allies for damages caused by the war. Wilson agreed to the Treaty of Versailles. However, the U.S. Senate argued that the treaty was too severe and would not support it.

■ PRACTICE 63: Woodrow Wilson and World War I

Decide if each statement below is true (**T**) or false (**F**). Write the correct letter on the line before each statement.

____ **1.** The FTC is responsible for overseeing foreign trade.

____ **2.** The Central Powers included Austria-Hungary, Germany, and Italy.

_____ **3.** The Allied Powers included France, Great Britain, Russia, and later the United States and Italy.

_____ **4.** President Wilson wanted to avoid entering World War I.

_____ **5.** In World War I, the Allies defeated the Central Powers.

THINK ABOUT IT

Everyone agrees that war is a terrible thing. It breaks up families, kills people, and costs a lot of money. Yet, sometimes war can have positive effects. In what ways do you think World War I might have been good for the United States? Write your answer on a separate sheet of paper.

After the War

Anti-Immigrant Feelings

When the war ended, factories had to switch from making war material to producing consumer goods. Many factories had to shut down, and unemployment was high. American workers were earning less than they had during the war. They also felt threatened by the large numbers of new immigrants. As you read earlier, laws were passed that restricted the numbers of immigrants. Some laws set quotas to limit the numbers of immigrants from certain countries.

Racial Unrest

During World War I, more than half a million African Americans moved to northern cities. They moved to find jobs in the factories that were busy making materials for war. When the war ended, though, African Americans faced discrimination from many returning veterans. White men who had fought in the war did not want to compete with blacks for jobs. Some white organizations stirred up hatred in the South and Midwest. They were responsible for many acts of racial violence. In 1919, there were race riots in 28 cities.

Women's Suffrage

Susan B. Anthony, a women's suffrage leader

Growing industrialization also led to more women in the workplace. This taste of economic freedom gave women the desire for more political freedom as well. The **women's suffrage movement** called for full voting rights for women. By 1914, women in 12 states had won the right to vote. In 1916, Montana elected the first woman to Congress. Finally, in 1920, the Nineteenth Amendment gave all American women the right to vote.

Prohibition

Since the early 1800s, there had been a temperance movement in the United States. Members of the **temperance movement** believed in a ban on all alcoholic drinks. They felt that many working men simply drank away what they earned, leaving their families poor and hungry. In 1919, the Eighteenth Amendment was passed. It banned the manufacture, sale, or transportation of alcoholic drinks. This act of Congress was called **Prohibition.** However, Prohibition was repealed, or canceled, by the Twenty-First Amendment, ratified in 1933.

PRACTICE 64: After the War

Circle the letter of the correct answer to each of the following questions.

1. Which amendment gave women the right to vote?
  - **a.** the Twenty-First Amendment
  - **b.** the Eighteenth Amendment
  - **c.** the Nineteenth Amendment
  - **d.** the Twentieth Amendment

2. Why did many African Americans move north after World War I?
  - **a.** They preferred the cooler climate.
  - **b.** They could get better jobs in the North.
  - **c.** They were escaping slavery in the South.
  - **d.** There was free farmland there.

The Roaring Twenties

The 1920s earned the name the **Roaring Twenties.** Indeed, for one ten-year period, it did seem as though America was roaring ahead. New technology and modern inventions made everyday living easier and created new jobs. Washing machines, electric lights, radios, cars, and tractors are just some of the things that improved American's lives.

One symbol of the new age was the automobile. At first, only the rich could afford cars. The average price of an American automobile in 1907 was $1,123. That was a lot of money at the time. Over time, though, mass production changed this. By 1924, Henry Ford's company could offer a car model for $540. By 1928, there were about 26 million cars on American roads. This began to change the face of America. The highway system grew. Roadside businesses multiplied. Tourism increased. Suburbs appeared and spread.

Another important development of the 1920s was commercial radio. By 1928, about 10 million families had at least one radio in their homes. People often sat together listening to the radio much as they now sit in front of a television set. Radio advertisements encouraged the sales of mass-produced goods. People also flocked to modern movie "palaces" and small-town movie theaters. They were drawn by popular screen stars.

As you have already learned, the Eighteenth Amendment was passed in 1919 to ban alcoholic drinks. In response to this law, illegal bars sprang up in every city. These bars were called **speakeasies.** They became a third symbol of the 1920s. As the illegal liquor trade grew, it became controlled by organized crime. Corrupt (dishonest) police and politicians would look the other way in exchange for money. People continued to drink as much as, or even more than, they had before Prohibition.

A style of music called jazz is another symbol of the 1920s. Jazz grew out of black spirituals, work songs, and European harmonies. In the 1920s, both black and white musicians were playing jazz. The **Jazz Age** ushered in new dances and a new style of dress. Daring women were wearing shorter skirts, smoking in public, and doing a dance called the Charleston.

IN REAL LIFE

Do you have a jazz club in your town or city? As you have just learned, jazz is a style of music that grew out of early black spirituals, work songs, and European harmonies. As African Americans moved north in the late 1800s and early 1900s, so did their music. Jazz became popular in such urban centers as Chicago and New York. By the late 1920s, jazz could be heard almost everywhere in the United States. The first great jazz musicians were African Americans. They included "Jelly Roll" Morton, Bessie Smith, and Louis Armstrong. Today, jazz is considered one of the few truly American art forms.

A final symbol of the 1920s is urbanization. This is the movement of people to the cities. The 1920 census, or population count, showed that for the first time in American history, there were more people living in cities than on farms and in other rural areas. Farmers who had done well before World War I fell into debt, as the war-torn nations of Europe started growing their own produce again. Many of these U.S. farmers had to leave their farms to find work in the cities.

PRACTICE 65: The Roaring Twenties

Circle the letter of the correct answer to each of the following questions.

1. What is another term for the 1920s?
- **a.** Prohibition
- **b.** urbanization
- **c.** the Roaring Twenties
- **d.** the Great Depression

2. What is the term for a shift in population from rural areas to cities?
- **a.** speakeasies
- **b.** imperialism
- **c.** arbitration
- **d.** urbanization

The Great Depression

Many people thought the good life of the 1920s would last forever. Yet, there were signs that the good times might be coming to an end. Workers' salaries did not keep up with rising prices. Workers could not even afford to buy the goods they made. Lower demand for goods caused factories to reduce production. In some cases, factories laid off workers. Even the automobile industry, which had been a huge success earlier in the decade, was also suffering.

Despite the signs of a slowdown, people continued to invest in the stock market. They would buy **stocks**, or shares of ownership in a company. The prices of stocks kept doubling. People would make money by buying when the price was low and selling when the price was high. By September 1929, stock prices were 400 percent higher than they had been 5 years earlier. Then on Tuesday, October 29, 1929, the stock market crashed. Everyone wanted to sell; no one wanted to buy. Prices fell fast. Many investors lost all their savings. This day was called **Black Tuesday**.

In the economic failures that followed, many workers lost their jobs. Nations all over the world were affected by what was called the Great Depression. As you learned in Lesson 9, when prices are depressed, or down, the economy slows down. There had been depressions before, but nothing quite matched this one. There were many reasons for it, including the following:

- Many countries were in debt because of World War I.
- Farmers' buying power (purchasing power) was down.
- Labor-saving machines meant fewer jobs for people, who now had less spending power.
- Goods remained unsold, so factories cut back on workers or even went out of business.
- Wealth was concentrated in the hands of a small number of people.
- People had less to spend because they had lost money in the stock market.
- A weak banking system meant that many banks closed when people withdrew (took out) their savings.

The Great Depression lasted for ten years. It was a sad finish to an exciting, productive period in American history. It ended only when the onset of World War II spurred new economic production.

PRACTICE 66: The Great Depression

Decide if each statement below is true (**T**) or false (**F**). Write the correct letter on the line before each statement.

_____ **1.** Before the stock market crashed, there were no signs of an economic slowdown.

_____ **2.** Many workers lost their jobs during the Great Depression.

_____ **3.** New labor-saving machines helped put more people to work.

_____ **4.** The Great Depression lasted through most of the 1930s.

TIP

Making a time line can help you see trends. A *trend* is a movement of things that are alike in some way. For example, look at these events on a time line of the 1920s:

1920 Growth of urban population

1920 Start of commercial radio

1925 Introduction of the Charleston

1928 26 million registered motor vehicles

1929 Stock market crashes on Black Tuesday

1929 Great Depression begins

Can you see a trend from this time line? The 1920s started off quickly, with many exciting developments. Then, toward the end, the Roaring Twenties crashed, along with the stock market.

LESSON 11: America from 1930 to 1945

GOAL: To identify the causes, results, and key people and events of the Great Depression and World War II

WORDS TO KNOW

amphibious	**pension**
Battle of the Coral Sea	**public works projects**
CCC	**Selective Service Act**
D-Day	**Social Security Act**
dictator	**totalitarian**
draft	**V-E Day**
Fair Labor Standards Act	**V-J Day**
Holocaust	**warlords**
New Deal	**Works Progress Administration (WPA)**

After the Stock Market Crash

When President Herbert Hoover took office early in 1929, he promised that the "abolition [end] of poverty" was close. Nine months later, the stock market crashed. By the end of 1929, the economy was sinking fast. Hoover did not believe the government should get involved. He feared that large government spending would be bad for business and would drive up prices. He did not like the idea of government interfering with business.

Herbert Hoover

Things got so bad, however, that Hoover finally had to act. He asked Congress to send money to the states for **public works projects** that would create jobs. These are large building and repair projects, such as repairing bridges and roads. The president also tried to help farmers and manufacturers by putting tariffs on imported goods. This made American goods cheaper than goods imported from other countries. Hoover hoped that this would encourage people to buy American-made products. He thought it would put more money into the U.S. economy. Unfortunately, the tariffs only made matters worse. Other countries reacted by adding their own tariffs to American goods. So, American goods no longer sold well in other countries.

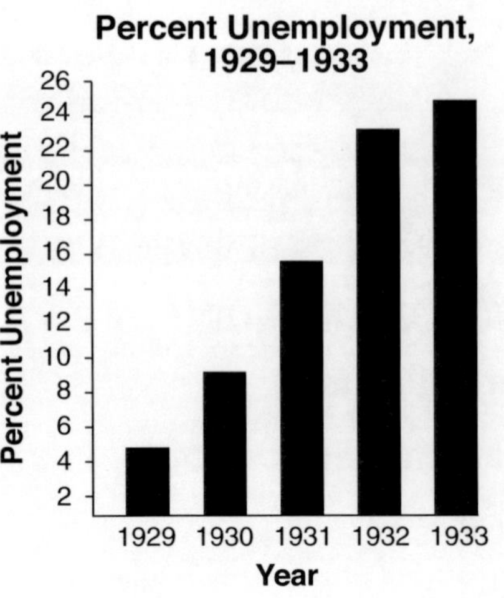

In fact, none of these measures worked. They were not extreme enough. Look at the graph above. It shows how unemployment grew between 1929 and 1933.

PRACTICE 67: After the Stock Market Crash

Decide if each statement below is true (**T**) or false (**F**). Write the correct letter on the line before each statement.

_____ **1.** From the start, President Hoover felt strongly that the government should take steps to improve the economy.

_____ **2.** Congress helped the states by sending money for public works projects.

The New Deal's First Hundred Days

On March 4, 1933, Franklin Delano Roosevelt, a Democrat, took office as president. Roosevelt was a fifth cousin of Theodore Roosevelt and the popular governor of New York. He promised a "new deal for the American people." He immediately set to work on his programs of relief, recovery, and reform.

The banks in America were in danger. Many banks were failing, because people wanted to withdraw all of the money from their savings accounts. People were worried that their savings were not safe. In fact, their deposits had been used to give other people loans. All the loans would have had to have been paid off at once to get enough money to cover the deposits. Roosevelt declared a four-day "bank holiday." All banks were closed. Only the healthy ones would open again, and the U.S. Treasury would manage some of them for a while.

Roosevelt called his program for recovery the **New Deal**. The program gave direct relief to state governments and individuals. Roosevelt and Congress set up agencies to put money into the hands of people who had none. Most of the agencies had long names: Federal Emergency Relief Administration, Civil Works Administration, Civilian Conservation Corps. They were all known by their initials: FERA, CWA, and CCC, for example. FERA gave money to state and local welfare agencies, which then gave the money to the unemployed. The CWA created jobs in construction. The **CCC** provided jobs for young men aged 18 to 25. They planted trees, built bridges, and created parks. More than 2.5 million men served in the CCC.

New Dealers believed that the central government should be more involved in planning and regulating (controlling) the economy. To help farmers, the government paid them to cut back on the size of their crops so that prices could rise. The government also enforced laws to make businesses follow certain standards, or rules. And, it brought cheap electricity to regions that did not have it.

PRACTICE 68: The New Deal's First Hundred Days

Decide if each statement below is true (**T**) or false (**F**). Write the correct letter on the line before each statement.

_____ **1.** Theodore Roosevelt promised a new deal for the American people.

_____ **2.** The CCC provided jobs for young men willing to plant trees, build bridges, and create parks.

_____ **3.** The government wanted farmers to grow more crops to feed the hungry people.

_____ **4.** New dealers were in favor of the government controlling the economy.

The New Deal: The Second Stage

The president and others realized that Americans needed work that was real and useful. The **Works Progress Administration (WPA)** was created in 1935 to give men and women jobs and a chance to help society. WPA projects used people with all sorts of skills: construction workers, librarians, teachers, actors, artists, and writers. Workers built schools and roads, put on theater performances and concerts, taught adults to read, and ran traveling libraries.

In 1935, probably one of the most important laws of the New Deal was passed. The **Social Security Act** gave states grants (large amounts of money) to care for children and those who could not work because of poor health. It paid for state unemployment insurance through a tax on workers and employers. It also set up a national system of pensions. A **pension** is a payment to someone who has retired because of age.

New Dealers believed that certain practices of big business had caused the Great Depression. To prevent any more economic crashes, big business needed to be regulated. This meant that they had to be made to follow *regulations,* or rules. Congress passed measures like the Securities and Exchange Act. It also passed laws to protect workers' rights. For example, the **Fair Labor Standards Act** of 1937 set up a minimum wage.

To pay for all the new programs, the government raised taxes. It raised taxes on individuals as well as businesses.

■ PRACTICE 69: The New Deal: The Second Stage

Circle the letter of the correct answer to each of the following questions.

1. Which of the following people might have had a job with the WPA?
   - **a.** a construction worker
   - **b.** an artist
   - **c.** a writer
   - **d.** all of the above

2. What is a pension?
    a. money paid to a prisoner
    b. money paid to someone too old to work
    c. a kind of hotel
    d. money paid to people too young to work

IN REAL LIFE

In the mid- to late 1990s, First Lady Hillary Rodham Clinton attracted much attention from the press. She was playing an active role in the administration of her husband, President Bill Clinton. While Mrs. Clinton had many critics, others applauded her for taking the role of First Lady in a new direction. Another First Lady who was both criticized and praised for her initiative was Eleanor Roosevelt, wife of President Franklin D. Roosevelt. While she was First Lady, Mrs. Roosevelt also served as a teacher, social reformer, and writer. She traveled to many places and reported on them to the president. One of Mrs. Roosevelt's greatest concerns was civil rights—the fight for equality for all people, regardless of skin color or ethnic background. After World War II, Mrs. Roosevelt served as the U.S. delegate to the United Nations. Many consider Eleanor Roosevelt to be the most effective first lady in U.S. history.

Eleanor Roosevelt

The New Deal Slows Down

By 1936, there were fewer big New Deal measures. As the economy slowly improved, there was more opposition to such legislation (laws). The New Deal was expensive. The new Social Security tax reduced paychecks and profits. Therefore, people bought and invested less. The economy slumped again in 1937. Two million more people were out of work by year's end.

Yet, even Roosevelt's harshest critics had to admit that he had accomplished a great deal. He had shown that the government could play an important role in keeping the economy and society stable. It had set minimum standards for public welfare and working conditions. It had helped the poor. And, it had protected the middle class against the worst effects of the Great Depression.

PRACTICE 70: The New Deal Slows Down

Decide if each statement below is true (**T**) or false (**F**). Write the correct letter on the line before each statement.

_____ **1.** The economy slumped again in 1937 because people had less money to spend.

_____ **2.** The New Deal did not do anything to help the poor.

_____ **3.** People had smaller paychecks because of Social Security taxes.

IN REAL LIFE

President Roosevelt's reforms still live on today. Americans can still collect Social Security and welfare payments from their state and federal governments. However, there have been changes in welfare laws. In 1996, President Bill Clinton signed the Welfare Reform Act. This act limits the number of years a person can collect welfare from the government. The goal was to encourage unemployed people to look for jobs. Another goal was for businesses to offer more training programs for people willing to work but in need of skills. In 2005, President George W. Bush led an effort to "privatize" Social Security. The goal of this effort was, in part, to take some of the burden for Social Security payments off the government's shoulders. People would be allowed to invest some of their money in private accounts instead of government accounts. President Bush believed that private investments could lead to greater returns (profits) on people's money.

Totalitarianism and War

While the United States was battling the Great Depression, much of Europe was falling under the control of totalitarian governments. In a **totalitarian** government, a dictator runs the country. A **dictator** is someone who has complete, or total, control. Totalitarianism does not permit anyone to disagree with government. In Italy, Benito Mussolini had risen to power after World War I. He declared himself dictator in 1926. In Germany, Adolf Hitler and his Nazi party had won total power over the German government in 1933. Furthermore, in Japan, military leaders called **warlords** had seized control in the 1920s.

The totalitarian rulers expressed their hatred for democracy. It was, in Mussolini's words, "a rotting corpse" that had to be replaced by "efficient" government and a "superior" way of life. The Nazis preached that the Germans were a master race with a mission (duty) to conquer Europe. Japan believed in its own racial superiority. It felt that its destiny was to rule all of Asia.

Germany had lost several territories with its defeat in World War I. Hitler and many Germans felt that the Treaty of Versailles, which had settled World War I, had unfairly punished them. In the 1930s, Germany started trying to take these territories back. The following time line shows the warlike steps the Axis powers (Germany, Italy, and Japan) took in the years leading up to World War II.

The world was stunned when Joseph Stalin, the dictator of communist Russia, signed an agreement with Hitler in 1939. Their agreement left Russia free to invade the Baltic nations of Latvia, Estonia, and Lithuania. Russia and Germany also divided Poland between them. England and France declared war on Germany. One by one, though, most of the countries of western Europe fell before the German *blitzkrieg* or "lightning war." Germany occupied (took over) Finland, Norway, Denmark, Holland, Belgium, Luxembourg, and finally France. The invasion of Great Britain (England) seemed to be next.

■ PRACTICE 71: Totalitarianism and War

Circle the letter of the correct answer to each of the following questions.

1. In what kind of government does one person have total control?
- **a.** democratic
- **b.** socialist
- **c.** totalitarian
- **d.** utopian

2. What kind of leader makes all the decisions on his or her own?
- **a.** a president
- **b.** a dictator
- **c.** a prime minister
- **d.** a mayor

Mobilizing the Home Front

The American people did not want to get involved in World War II. In 1935, Congress passed a law that allowed the president to stop the sale of weapons to warring nations. As the Axis powers seized more territory, though, it became harder for the United States to remain neutral. President Roosevelt persuaded Congress to let him send the Allies (Great Britain, France, and China) military supplies. Meanwhile, the United States began to build up its own military forces. In September 1940, Congress passed the **Selective Service Act**, the first peacetime draft in American history. A **draft** is a mandatory (required) call to enroll in the armed forces. The United States still hoped to stay neutral. Yet, little by little, the country was mobilizing (getting ready) for war.

In 1940, England was under attack by the Germans. From September 1940 until May 1941, German bombs fell on London every night. Despite the assaults, British Prime Minister Winston Churchill promised never to surrender to the Germans. English radar technology, and the courage of both the military and civilians, was holding off the Germans. However, the English could not replace the equipment they had lost. President Roosevelt very much wanted to help the English. In early 1941, Congress passed the Lend-Lease Act. As you learned in Lesson 9, this act allowed the president to sell, trade, lend, or lease war materials to any country whose defense was vital to the defense of the United States.

In the spring of 1941, tension continued to mount. German and Italian submarines were trying to sink American ships in the Atlantic. They wanted to keep supplies from reaching England. In September, Roosevelt issued a "shoot-on-sight" order. Soon, U.S. warships began to convoy (accompany) U.S. merchant ships as far as Iceland. Two months later, the U.S. warships started to enter combat areas. To many people, it looked as if the United States was very close to declaring war.

PRACTICE 72: Mobilizing the Home Front

Decide if each statement below is true (**T**) or false (**F**). Write the correct letter on the line before each statement.

_____ **1.** Great Britain, France, and China were part of the Axis powers.

_____ **2.** Another term for the Selective Service is the draft.

_____ **3.** President Roosevelt did not want to help the British in their fight against the Germans.

_____ **4.** The Lend-Lease Act allowed the United States to send weapons to some countries in the war.

America Goes to War

As you learned earlier, on December 7, 1941, Japan launched a surprise attack on Pearl Harbor, Hawaii. This was the home of America's Pacific fleet. In all, Japanese airplanes sank or disabled 19 ships, including 2 battleships. They destroyed 150 planes and killed 2,400 soldiers and sailors. The U.S. Navy's aircraft carriers survived only because they were at sea at the time.

Following this attack on American territory, the United States officially declared war on Japan. On December 11, Germany and Italy declared war on the United States.

The United States was now faced with powerful enemies on two sides—the Atlantic and the Pacific. The president and his advisers decided that they must first defeat the Nazis. Meanwhile, Germany was still on the move in 1941. German forces that year attacked Egypt, Yugoslavia, Greece, and Crete. In June, ignoring the pact he had signed, Hitler attacked Russia. Instead of remaining neutral, Russia now needed Allied help. The question was whether the Russians could hold out until American and British supplies reached them.

The heroic Russian forces went on to defeat the Germans. For the first time since they started to roll across Europe in their tanks, the German forces were stopped. What was left of the German army in Russia surrendered in January 1943. Then, Russian forces started advancing, or moving toward, Germany.

Meanwhile in Africa, British and American forces were driving the Germans away. In 1943, the German troops in Africa were forced to surrender.

Roosevelt and Churchill decided to invade Europe where the enemy was weakest—in Italy. In July and August of 1943, British and American forces began moving into Italy. They forced the overthrow (defeat) of Mussolini. However, the Germans continued to battle. It was not until June 1944 that the German forces in Italy surrendered.

American and British air forces were engaged in "round-the-clock" bombing of German industry and transportation. The only real way to defeat the German army, though, was on the ground. On **D-Day**, June 6, 1944, the greatest amphibious force in history landed on the coast of Normandy (northwestern France). An **amphibious** force is one that arrives by sea but can operate on land. By September, the Allies had reached the western border of Germany. Meanwhile, the Russians were closing in from the east.

May 8, 1945, was **V-E Day** (Victory in Europe Day). Germany had surrendered to the Allies. Hitler, however, was already dead. He had killed himself rather than face the victorious Allied armies. Millions of happy Americans celebrated the German surrender.

PRACTICE 73: America Goes to War

Circle the letter of the correct answer to each of the following questions.

1. Why did Russia become an ally of the United States instead of remaining neutral?

- **a.** because the Germans attacked Russia
- **b.** because the Americans had a stronger military force
- **c.** because the Russians wanted to try American food
- **d.** because they knew the United States would win the war

2. Where did the D-Day invasion take place?

- **a.** in Germany
- **b.** in France
- **c.** in Italy
- **d.** in Africa

3. Which country surrendered on V-E Day?

- **a.** the United States
- **b.** England
- **c.** Germany
- **d.** Japan

The Defeat of Japan

Even after Germany surrendered, the war with Japan continued. Japan had taken over American bases in Guam and Wake Island. It also had taken the British colony of Hong Kong and all of Thailand. Singapore, the Philippines, most of Burma, and the East Indies fell to Japanese troops. Then, however, the war began to turn against the Japanese. The Allies used planes and submarines to drive them back. In May 1942, there was a turning point. An American naval force defeated a Japanese fleet in the **Battle of the Coral Sea**. Meanwhile, U.S. naval forces continued to grow quickly. The Japanese, though, could not replace all the ships they had lost.

With Germany's surrender, the Allies could concentrate all their forces against Japan. Still, many more lives would be lost in the effort to beat the Japanese. Vice President Harry Truman had become president when Roosevelt died in April 1945. He learned that Roosevelt had ordered a powerful new weapon called the atom bomb. To shorten the war, Truman ordered that a bomb be dropped on the Japanese city of Hiroshima on August 6. On August 9, a second bomb fell on the city of Nagasaki. The bombs killed more than 150,000 Japanese. Thousands more were injured from the radiation. Fearing total destruction, the Japanese surrendered. The day on which the fighting officially stopped, August 15, 1945, is known as **V-J Day** (Victory in Japan).

■ PRACTICE 74: The Defeat of Japan

Decide if each statement below is true (**T**) or false (**F**). Write the correct letter on the line before each statement.

_____ **1.** Japan and Germany surrendered on the same day, V-E Day.

_____ **2.** President Harry Truman made the decision to drop the atomic bomb on Japan.

_____ **3.** The Japanese surrendered because they feared the United States would drop more atomic bombs on them.

The High Cost of Hatred

While there was much joy over the end of a terrible war, there was also deep sadness at the costs of the war. Americans learned the truth about what had taken place in Europe under the Nazis. In his writings, Adolf Hitler had described Germans as a "master race" that should rule the world. Any group that he felt was "inferior" was to be totally destroyed.

Hitler's main targets were Jews. He also ordered that many other people, such as Gypsies, homosexuals, and people with disabilities, be rounded up and killed. Under his orders, millions of people—men, women, and children—were murdered in death camps. Those who did not die right away were used for slave labor.

It was not until Allied forces liberated, or freed, the survivors of the death camps that many Americans fully understood what had happened. In newsreels at movie theaters across the country, they saw the starving survivors of this nightmare. They learned that more than 6 million Jews had died in what was called the **Holocaust**, the mass slaughter, or killing, of a people.

The total loss of lives in World War II in Europe was so high that the numbers are hard to understand. The following figures are only military losses for some of the countries involved in the war:

Soviet Union	8.6 million
Germany	3.2 million
China	1.3 million
Japan	1.5 million
Great Britain	0.3 million
France	0.3 million
United States	0.3 million

With much of Europe and Asia in ruins, continental America was untouched. It emerged from the war as a major world power, with its economy strong and its democracy safe.

PRACTICE 75: The High Cost of Hatred

Decide if each statement below is true (**T**) or false (**F**). Write the correct letter on the line before each statement. Then answer question 4.

_____ **1.** The word *holocaust* means "mass murder of a people."

_____ **2.** At the end of the war, the U.S. economy was weaker due to the war effort.

_____ **3.** Many millions of people were killed in World War II.

4. Hiroshima and Nagasaki were completely destroyed by the atomic bombs. Japan surrendered, bringing World War II to an end. What were the main arguments—for and against—dropping the bombs on Japan? Do you think it was right to use the atomic bomb? Explain your answer below.

____

____

____

____

____

____

____

____

____

LESSON 12: America from 1945 to the Present

GOAL: To demonstrate knowledge of historical events, people, and trends in American history since World War II

WORDS TO KNOW

baby boom

boycott

capitalist economy

Civil Rights Act of 1957

Cold War

Commonwealth of Independent States

communist

conservatives

consumer goods

GI Bill

Iron Curtain

liberals

limited war

Marshall Plan

National Aeronautics and Space Administration (NASA)

North Atlantic Treaty Organization (NATO)

racial discrimination

Soviet Union

Sputnik

superpowers

thirty-eighth parallel

Vietnam

Warsaw Pact

The Cold War

After World War II, the world shifted. New relationships were forged between nations. The United States emerged as a major world power. How would the nation handle its new role in the coming decades? This lesson will explore the events and developments of U.S. history from 1945 to the present.

The world's two great powers at the end of World War II were the Soviet Union and the United States. They were called the two **superpowers**.

Once allies, they became enemies almost as soon as the last shot of the war was fired. Joseph Stalin was the Soviet premier (top leader). He began to install Soviet-controlled governments in the countries Russia had occupied at the end of the war. This group of countries, with Russia, became the **Soviet Union.** Stalin tried to isolate these countries from the rest of the world. British Prime Minister Winston Churchill said it was as though an "iron curtain" had been drawn between the West and Russian territory. The West often did not know what was going on behind this imaginary line called the **Iron Curtain.**

Soviet-controlled territories after World War II

The United States is a democracy with a **capitalist economy.** People have the right to own businesses and land. They also have freedom of speech and expression. The Soviet Union, however, was a communist country. In a **communist** country, people are supposed to share ownership of most things. However, the Soviet Union also had a totalitarian government. This means that the government controlled everything: education, travel, religion, books, art, sports, and even music.

Stalin declared that true international peace was impossible "under the present capitalist development of the world economy." Many people on the other side of the Iron Curtain were alarmed by Stalin's statements. Their fear grew when they learned that the Soviet Union was building its own atomic weapons.

The U.S. government thought that Stalin wanted to place communist governments in more countries around the world. In 1947, U.S. President Harry Truman asked Congress for money to support countries threatened by communism. In response, Congress passed the Marshall Plan. The **Marshall Plan**, named after Secretary of State George Marshall, sent billions of dollars to help European countries recover from the war. The money was also intended to help those countries fight the threat of communism. The Soviet Union and its satellites (Eastern European countries under its control) refused to take part. But, Western Europe recovered quickly with the help of American dollars.

In 1949, Western nations formed the **North Atlantic Treaty Organization**, known as **NATO**. The NATO countries agreed that an attack against one would be considered an attack against all. The Soviet Union and its satellite countries responded in the same way. They formed their own group called the **Warsaw Pact**.

Thus began what was called the **Cold War**. The two great powers, the United States and the Soviet Union, never had an actual war. Yet, the battles of the Cold War would control foreign policy for the next 40 years.

PRACTICE 76: The Cold War

Decide if each statement below is true (**T**) or false (**F**). Write the correct letter on the line before each statement.

_____ **1.** A capitalist economy is one in which people can own their businesses and land.

_____ **2.** The Iron Curtain was an iron fence built to separate the Soviet Union from European countries.

_____ **3.** The Marshall Plan sent money to nations in the Soviet Union.

_____ **4.** NATO was formed by Western nations that wanted to protect one another from military threats.

On the Home Front

After the war, the U.S. economy thrived. Manufacturers had the materials and workers to make the **consumer goods** people wanted: cars, houses, furniture, clothes. For many returning veterans, it was time to settle down and raise families. The population grew very fast in what became known as the **baby boom**.

Veterans got a boost from a 1944 law known as the GI Bill. (GI stands for "government issue." Soldiers jokingly used this term to refer to themselves.) The **GI Bill** provided veterans with unemployment insurance, loans to build homes and start businesses, medical treatment, job training, and education. This bill put $13 billion into the U.S. economy.

World War II also brought about changes for women. Many women worked during the war or served in the armed forces. When the male veterans came home, they took jobs back from many female workers. Women, however, had grown used to paychecks. There were openings in "women's work" to replace jobs lost to the veterans. But, these jobs paid less than the men's.

Another group affected by World War II was African Americans. Before the war, in the 1940s, many black Americans had moved north. More blacks were in higher-paying jobs than ever before. However, their wages were still lower than those of white males. They were also more likely to lose their jobs when any layoffs had to be made. In northern cities, black housing was usually limited to one section of the city. In the South, the practice of segregation—keeping races apart—continued.

Many African Americans had served in the armed forces, in segregated units. These men had risked their lives to defend their country and liberate their Allies. Yet, they often returned to the same conditions they had left, especially in the South. There were still many incidents of hate crimes against blacks. Change was coming, but it was slow. In 1948, President Truman ordered the military to be fully *integrated,* or open to anyone. He also banned **racial discrimination** (unfairness based on race) in hiring for federal jobs.

PRACTICE 77: On the Home Front

Circle the letter of the correct answer to each of the following questions.

1. What law helped returning veterans settle into civilian life?
    - **a.** the Marshall Plan
    - **b.** the GI Bill
    - **c.** the baby boom
    - **d.** unemployment insurance

2. What term names the practice of separating people of different races?
    - **a.** integration
    - **b.** discrimination
    - **c.** segregation
    - **d.** equality

IN REAL LIFE

Have you heard of the NAACP? Some of your friends, family members, and neighbors may be members of this organization. The letters *NAACP* stand for the National Association for the Advancement of Colored People. The NAACP was formed in 1909 to end segregation and racial inequality. Many of the legal cases the NAACP has fought have served as turning points in the history of American civil rights.

The Korean War

At the end of World War II, Korea was divided into two parts. A communist government took over in the north, a capitalist government in the south. On June 25, 1950, North Korea invaded South Korea. The United Nations asked member nations to help South Korea "repel the armed attack." The United States was a leading member of the United Nations. President Truman ordered the U.S. armed forces to "keep the peace" in Korea.

The U.N. forces started driving the North Korean forces out of South Korea. Then communist China stepped in to help North Korea. Hundreds of thousands of Chinese soldiers pushed the U.N. troops back. President Truman then decided to wage a limited war. A **limited war** meant that the main goal was not to win the war but to restore the boundary between North Korea and South Korea. In a limited war, nuclear weapons are not used.

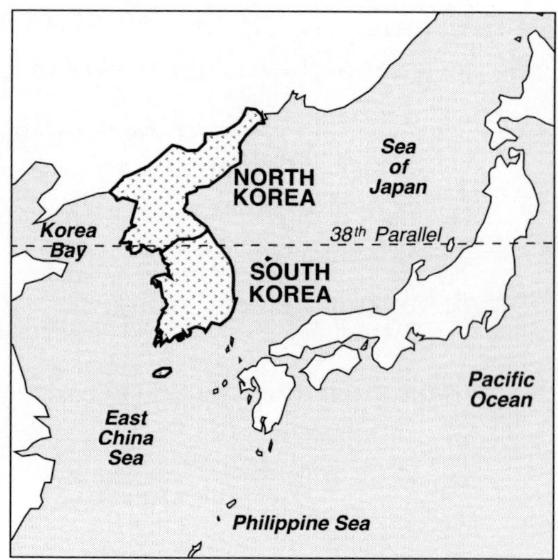

North Korea and South Korea

In 1952, General Dwight D. Eisenhower was elected president of the United States. Eisenhower was determined to bring an end to the Korean War. In July 1953, a cease-fire was signed. The **thirty-eighth parallel** was restored as the boundary between communist North Korea and capitalist South Korea. More than 1.5 million Americans and South Koreans had died in the war. China and North Korea lost the same number.

PRACTICE 78: The Korean War

Circle the letter of the correct answer to each of the following questions.

1. When did the conflict in Korea begin?
- **a.** when South Korea invaded North Korea
- **b.** when China sided with North Korea
- **c.** when North Korea invaded South Korea
- **d.** when President Truman was elected

2. Why was the thirty-eighth parallel important?
- **a.** It was where all the battles took place.
- **b.** It served as the boundary between North Korea and South Korea.
- **c.** It was where the cease-fire was signed.
- **d.** It was the only place where the Chinese would fight.

The Eisenhower Years

Dwight D. Eisenhower, a Republican, was the thirty-fourth president of the United States. He had been the commander of the Allied forces in World War II. After the war, he had headed NATO. When Eisenhower became president, the United States wanted a return to "normalcy." Generally, the 1950s were peaceful at home.

But, the Cold War had an effect on domestic life. Some people feared that communists were trying to infiltrate (get inside of) American institutions and overthrow the government. Senator Joseph McCarthy led a series of investigations against Americans suspected of being communists. Some of these people went to prison. Many of the accusations, however, could not be proved. Still, they could easily destroy a person's career.

Dwight D. Eisenhower

Despite the relative peace of the 1950s, it was also a time when the fight for civil rights heated up. In 1954, the U.S. Supreme Court ruled on a case known as *Brown v. Board of Education of Topeka.* (The v. stands for versus, which means "against or opposed to.") The question before the court was whether having separate schools for blacks and whites was constitutional if those schools were "equal." The court ruled that separate schools could not, by definition, be equal. Schools had to be integrated.

In 1955, Rosa Parks, a black woman, was arrested in Montgomery, Alabama. She had refused to give up her seat on a bus to a white man. Parks was sitting in the front of the bus. African Americans were supposed to move to the back of the bus if a white person needed a seat. Dr. Martin Luther King, Jr., led Montgomery blacks in a year-long boycott of the bus company. In a **boycott**, people protest what a certain business is doing by refusing to use that business. The Supreme Court declared that in buses, just as in schools, separate was *not* equal. This ruling gave blacks equal rights to public transportation.

Eisenhower ran for reelection in 1956. To win the black vote, he pushed the **Civil Rights Act of 1957** through Congress. This act expanded the power of the U.S. government to enforce voting rights. The president also sent in federal troops to enforce school desegregation in Little Rock, Arkansas.

■ PRACTICE 79: The Eisenhower Years

Decide if each statement below is true (**T**) or false (**F**). Write the correct letter on the line before each statement.

_____ **1.** The 1950s were a fairly peaceful time in the United States.

_____ **2.** A boycott is when a group of people refuse to go to work.

_____ **3.** In 1954, the Supreme Court ruled that it was legal to have separate (but equal) public schools for blacks and whites.

The Race for Space and the Kennedy Years

In October 1957, the Soviet Union launched ***Sputnik,*** a space satellite. Americans feared that this was a sign of the Soviet's lead in technology. Some people thought that the Soviets might use the same rockets to launch nuclear (atomic) missiles at American cities. Many Americans also felt that their own education system lagged behind the Soviet system. They thought that U.S. schools needed to focus more on math and science. In response, the United States sped up its own missile program. It encouraged science education and set up **NASA**, the **National Aeronautics and Space Administration.** NASA would promote both manned and unmanned space flights. To Americans, it was a "race for space." Space was now the new frontier. As a result, the United States finally landed astronauts on the moon in 1969.

In 1960, John F. Kennedy was elected president of the United States. Kennedy proposed many economic and social changes during his presidency. However, in 1963, Kennedy was assassinated (killed). At the time of his death, many of the bills he had proposed were stalled in Congress. Vice President Lyndon Johnson took over as president after Kennedy's death. Johnson saw that Kennedy's bills moved through Congress. Some examples of these bills are listed on the next page.

John F. Kennedy

- **Economic Opportunity Act of 1964:** provided education, job training, and employment programs for the poor
- **Medicaid, Medicare:** helped pay hospital and doctor bills of the poor and elderly
- **Housing legislation:** provided homes for low-income families
- **Civil Rights Act of 1964:** stopped discrimination in public places; fought employment discrimination
- **Voting Rights Act of 1965:** stressed the constitutional right of blacks to vote

PRACTICE 80: The Race for Space and the Kennedy Years

Check each statement below that is TRUE.

☐ **1.** NASA was formed in response to the launch of *Sputnik*.

☐ **2.** Many of President Kennedy's proposals for social change were passed by President Johnson.

The War in Vietnam

Despite his successes on the home front, Johnson was getting deeper and deeper into a distant war in Vietnam. **Vietnam** is a country in Southeast Asia. It was under French rule until 1954. When the French pulled out, the country was divided into two parts, North Vietnam and South Vietnam. The north was led by a communist government. The south was a democracy. The United States became involved because it wanted to preserve democracy in the south.

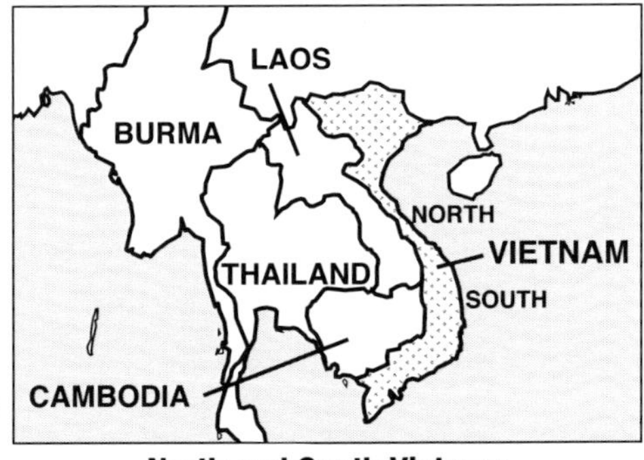

North and South Vietnam

The communist Vietcong were fighting to overthrow the government in South Vietnam. President Kennedy had sent U.S. military advisers and equipment there. They were trying to help the South Vietnamese defend themselves against the Vietcong. By the time Johnson became president, there were already 16,000 U.S. troops in Vietnam.

Bit by bit, America's role in the war grew. By the end of 1968, 536,000 U.S. troops were in Vietnam. More than 25,000 Americans had been killed. The U.S. government was spending billions of dollars on the war.

At home, many people believed that the United States should not be involved in Vietnam. Their feelings were influenced by nightly newscasts, which often showed disturbing war scenes. Many college students protested the war. Some of these protests led to violence.

Finally, in 1973, President Richard Nixon ordered all U.S. combat troops pulled out of Vietnam. The South Vietnamese were left to fight alone. By April 1975, the North Vietnamese had taken over South Vietnam.

The Vietnam War was a turning point for Americans. Many people stopped believing that the United States could use its strength to solve any problem in the world.

■ PRACTICE 81: The War in Vietnam

Decide if each statement below is true (**T**) or false (**F**). Write the correct letter on the line before each statement.

_____ **1.** The Vietcong fought to overthrow the government of South Vietnam.

_____ **2.** President Lyndon Johnson started sending U.S. advisers and equipment to Vietnam.

_____ **3.** The United States won the war in Vietnam.

THINK ABOUT IT

Involvement in the Vietnam War created a division among the people of the United States. Some felt that it was their duty to serve in the war. Others felt that America should stay out of Vietnam and let the Vietnamese fight their own battles. Some people even fled to Canada to avoid being drafted. What would you have done? How would you have felt about the Vietnam War? Write your answer on a separate sheet of paper.

The Reagan Years

In the 1980s, a new conservative mood swept the country. **Conservatives** believe that the government should *not* play a large role in solving social problems. **Liberals**, on the other hand, believe that the government *should* play a large role in solving social problems. President Ronald Reagan, a conservative Republican, wanted to build up the military. He meant to show the Soviet Union that the United States was strong. Under his direction, Congress spent huge amounts of money to build weapons.

In 1985, Mikhail Gorbachev became leader of the U.S.S.R. (the Soviet Union). Gorbachev recognized that the Soviet Union had problems. The military buildup, the cost of controlling satellite countries, and poor management were pulling down the Soviet economy. He called for cuts in military spending. He talked of friendship between the Warsaw Pact nations and the countries of the West.

Reagan and Gorbachev worked together to cut back on missiles and nuclear weapons. Both nations already had enough weapons.

Most Soviets welcomed Gorbachev's changes. But, Soviet leaders soon realized that it was hard to maintain limits on the new freedoms. Three republics that had been forced into the Soviet Union—Estonia, Latvia, and Lithuania—broke away and became independent countries. All over Eastern Europe, there were stirrings of freedom.

By 1991, Hungary, Poland, Czechoslovakia, Romania, and Bulgaria were free countries. In place of the Soviet Union, there was now the **Commonwealth of Independent States**. This was a union of equal, independent republics.

■ PRACTICE 82: The Reagan Years

Decide if each statement below is true (**T**) or false (**F**). Write the correct letter on the line before each statement.

_____ **1.** A conservative believes that the government should play a major role in solving social problems.

_____ **2.** Soviet leader Mikhail Gorbachev wanted to increase military spending.

_____ **3.** After the breakup of the Soviet Union, countries such as Hungary, Poland, and Bulgaria became free.

IN REAL LIFE

The Cold War began just as World War II came to an end. In 1990, the Cold War ended. When free speech became possible, the countries of the U.S.S.R. demanded freedom. Today, some of these countries are still struggling with their independence. Many U.S. companies have offices in these countries.

Social Change and the Clinton Years

The years after 1945 were a time of great change. The roles of women, for example, changed dramatically after World War II. In the 1960s and 1970s, the women's movement called attention to discrimination (prejudice) against women. Women demanded equal pay and fairness in hiring. By the 1980s and 1990s, many women held jobs that were once held only by men. Men were also now freer to train for careers once thought of as "women's work," such as nursing. At the same time, there was more recognition of the important roles of homemakers and child-care providers. Some men began to take the central role in child care while their wives worked.

Still, many issues of sexism, racism, and unequal pay remained unsolved. Drug use was still a problem. People shared many concerns about violence, homelessness, and the environment. There were questions about how these problems could, and should, be solved. Should the government take a larger part? The answers were mixed. In fact, the

American public has elected several divided governments since 1990. This means that the president belongs to one political party, while the majority of the Congress belongs to another. William Jefferson (Bill) Clinton was elected president in 1992. He was reelected in 1996. Clinton was the first Democrat to win a second term since Franklin D. Roosevelt. Yet, the majority in Congress was still Republican.

In his second term, President Clinton was accused of lying under oath about a sex scandal. In December of 1998, the House of Representatives moved to impeach the president. To *impeach* is to accuse a political official of wrongdoing. At the trial in early 1999, the Senate fell short of the votes needed to convict the president. Clinton stayed in office and apologized for his actions.

Throughout the 1990s, the United States continued to be involved in world affairs. Although many believed that there was no longer a threat of major war, there were some limited conflicts around the world. Happily, nuclear weapons were not part of any war in the 1990s. Their frightening power to destroy continued to keep all sides from using them. The memory of the Vietnam War also prevented the United States from becoming involved in another country's civil war. However, the United States did take part in the (Persian) Gulf War of 1990. During this war, the United States, under President George H. W. Bush, got other countries to help push back Iraq's attack on Kuwait. President Clinton also used force in Iraq in 1998. He ordered U.S. ships to fire missiles (bombs) at the country when the Iraqi dictator, Saddam Hussein, would not cooperate with U.N. weapons inspectors. American and British attacks destroyed much of Iraq's military power.

PRACTICE 83: Social Change and the Clinton Years

Decide if each statement below is true (**T**) or false (**F**). Write the correct letter on the line before each statement.

_____ **1.** The United States became involved in the Gulf War to push Kuwait out of Iraq.

_____ **2.** The United States solved most of its social problems in the 1990s.

The Dawn of the Twenty-First Century

The presidential election of 2000 was one of the closest in U.S. history. In fact, the U.S. Supreme Court played a major role in deciding the election. This was because in Florida, many Democrats wanted a vote recount in some key counties. Most Republicans were opposed to this idea. It looked as if the Democratic candidate, Vice President Al Gore, would win if the recount took place. In the end, the Court said that the recount could not occur. Therefore, the Republican candidate, George W. Bush, won the state of Florida. This, in turn, helped him to win the presidency.

Bush's first term was filled with problems. Once again, the country was divided. Democrats had bitter feelings about the Florida vote. Conservatives and liberals seemed more opposed than ever. However, this all changed on September 11, 2001, when the United States came under attack. Two passenger airplanes were flown into the two towers of the World Trade Center in New York City. At about the same time, another passenger plane hit the Pentagon (U.S. military headquarters) in Washington, D.C. A fourth passenger plane, which was also heading for Washington, crashed in Pennsylvania when a group of passengers fought with the men who had hijacked the plane. Nearly 3,000 people died in the September 11 attacks.

The enemy on that day did not turn out to be a nation. Instead, it was a group of Arab terrorists. They had a common goal: to destroy the economic and military power of the United States. The United States was at war, but this time it was a "global war on terror."

President Bush ordered U.S. forces to invade Afghanistan. This country borders Iran and Pakistan. Many terrorists had attended training camps there run by Osama bin Laden, a wealthy Saudi Arabian known for hating Western cultures. The training camps were destroyed by American bombs, and many suspected terrorists were captured. However, bin Laden escaped.

In 2003, President Bush ordered the invasion of Iraq. He claimed that Saddam Hussein was helping terrorists and building nuclear and other deadly weapons. In March 2003, the United States and some allies invaded Iraq. By April, the government of Saddam Hussein had fallen. However, the United States was unable to keep the peace in Iraq. Fighters opposed to the U.S. invasion and occupation of Iraq killed many U.S. troops. They also killed foreign workers and Iraqi civilians. They often targeted Iraqis who worked with the U.S.-led occupation forces and emerging Iraqi government. In the United States, people were divided about the conflict in Iraq.

In spite of these issues, President Bush was reelected in 2004. The nation still faced numerous problems. The global war on terror was still raging, and American troops were still in Iraq. At home, the economy was weaker. During the Bush years, the nation's debt ballooned. Also, people were divided about many social issues. The early years of the twenty-first century were filled with challenges.

PRACTICE 84: The Dawn of the Twenty-First Century

Circle the letter of the correct answer to each of the following questions.

1. Which group helped to decide the 2000 presidential election?
   a. the U.S. Senate
   b. the U.S. House of Representatives
   c. the Supreme Court
   d. the Pentagon

2. Who was responsible for the attacks of September 11, 2001?
   a. a group of Arab terrorists
   b. the kingdom of Saudi Arabia
   c. the nation of Afghanistan
   d. Saddam Hussein

3. Why did the United States invade Afghanistan in 2001?
   a. because Osama bin Laden, the country's leader, needed to be removed from office
   b. because there were terrorist training camps there
   c. both *a* and *b*
   d. neither *a* nor *b*

UNIT 4 REVIEW

Circle the letter of the correct answer to each of the following questions.

1. Why did the United States get involved in imperialism?
   - **a.** to find raw materials and markets for its products
   - **b.** to free Spanish colonies
   - **c.** to end a policy of neutrality
   - **d.** to help poor people throughout the world

2. What was the Great Depression?
   - **a.** a period when the economy grew quickly
   - **b.** a war between the United States and Europe
   - **c.** a period when the economy slowed down
   - **d.** a period of unrest between workers and bosses

3. What was the main reason why President Herbert Hoover could not stop the Great Depression?
   - **a.** The stock market was closed.
   - **b.** Prices were too high.
   - **c.** Farmers charged too much for what they produced.
   - **d.** He did not believe in government intervention.

4. Why did President Roosevelt ask farmers to cut back production?
   - **a.** because food cost too much
   - **b.** because most people were growing their own food
   - **c.** because it would raise crop prices
   - **d.** because labor laws for farmworkers were too strict

5. What was the purpose of the Lend-Lease Act?
   - **a.** to destroy German subs
   - **b.** to allow American ships to enter combat zones
   - **c.** to help Germany take over Russia
   - **d.** to help England defend itself against Germany

6. What was the purpose of the Marshall Plan?
   - **a.** to part the Iron Curtain
   - **b.** to solve the need for economic aid in Europe
   - **c.** to take Joseph Stalin out of power
   - **d.** all of the above

7. Why did the United States get involved in another war in 1950?
   - **a.** because China attacked South Korea
   - **b.** because a NATO country was attacked
   - **c.** because the Soviet Union crossed the thirty-eighth parallel
   - **d.** because North Korea attacked South Korea

8. What was the importance of the case *Brown v. Board of Education of Topeka*?
   - **a.** It said that separate schools could not be equal.
   - **b.** It ended the career of President John F. Kennedy.
   - **c.** It sent troops to Montgomery, Alabama.
   - **d.** It led to a bus boycott.

9. Why did the United States get involved in Vietnam?
   - **a.** President Nixon ordered American troops to go there.
   - **b.** The French asked America to step in.
   - **c.** The United States was helping the noncommunists against the communists.
   - **d.** The United States was helping South Korea take over communist Vietnam.

10. What did President Reagan and Mikhail Gorbachev work together to do?
    - **a.** improve social conditions
    - **b.** bring freedom to Soviet States
    - **c.** cut back on weapons
    - **d.** none of the above

UNIT 4 APPLICATION ACTIVITY 1

The Events of a Decade

Each decade (ten-year period) of the twentieth century had its exciting moments. There were, for example, the Roaring Twenties, World War II and the postwar years of the 1940s, and the rebellious 1960s.

Choose any one decade of the twentieth century. Make a list of six events that occurred during that decade. They should be things that were important enough to affect the future. For example, one event could be Wilbur and Orville Wright's first airplane flight in 1903. You can use the Internet, encyclopedias, world almanacs, and other reference books to find information about the decade you choose. If you choose a more recent decade, you can also interview someone who was alive during that decade. List your six events below.

Decade: ______________________________

1. ______________________________

2. ______________________________

3. ______________________________

4. ______________________________

5. ______________________________

6. ______________________________

After you make your list, mark and label the six events on the time line below. Write the year and a brief description of each event. (You can write on either side of the line.)

19___ 19___

UNIT 4 APPLICATION ACTIVITY 2

The Spoken Word

Speeches have been used for both good and evil. The lie-filled rantings of Hitler moved people to do cruel things. The peaceful, hopeful words of Dr. Martin Luther King, Jr., brought out the best qualities of many listeners.

Luckily, several speeches of the twentieth century have been preserved electronically. This allows you to listen to and/or watch many great men and women of the past. You can be inspired by their words, just as their first audiences were.

Use your local library to locate a civil rights speech of the twentieth century. Listen to it on audiotape or CD. Or, watch it on video or DVD. Find the words in the speech that most inspire you. Copy them on the lines below.

____

____

____

____

____

____

____

____

Now, use the ideas you heard, as well as your own, to prepare your own speech on the topic of civil rights. The speech should have three parts:

- a review of milestones (important events) in the struggle for civil rights
- quotations from other civil rights leaders (Be sure to give credit to the original speaker. For example, say, "In the words of . . . ".)
- your dreams for the future of civil rights

Write your speech on a separate sheet of paper.

UNIT 4 APPLICATION ACTIVITY 3

The Twenty-First Century

Congratulations! You are reaching the end of your study of United States history. In the future, you will be living through other periods of history. Someday, others will be studying those periods. What will they be learning?

Below and on the next page is a list of several topics that you have studied. In the space below each topic, write your predictions about what will happen during the rest of the twenty-first century.

Before you start writing, think about today's current events. Search the Internet, watch the news on television, and read newspapers and journals. This will help you predict tomorrow's history.

- **Immigration**

____

____

____

____

____

____

- **International Affairs**

____

____

____

____

____

____

■ The Economy

■ Civil Rights

■ Other Areas

APPENDIXES

A. Chronological List of Presidents

Washington, George	1789–97	Harrison, Benjamin	1889–93
Adams, John	1797–1801	Cleveland, Grover	1893–97
Jefferson, Thomas	1801–09	McKinley, William	1897–1901
Madison, James	1809–17	Roosevelt, Theodore	1901–09
Monroe, James	1817–25	Taft, William H.	1909–13
Adams, John	1825–29	Wilson, Woodrow	1913–21
Jackson, Andrew	1829–37	Harding, Warren	1921–23
Van Buren, Martin	1837–41	Coolidge, Calvin	1923–29
Harrison, William Henry	1841	Hoover, Herbert	1929–33
Tyler, John	1841–45	Roosevelt, Franklin D.	1933–45
Polk, James	1845–49	Truman, Harry	1945–53
Taylor, Zachary	1849–50	Eisenhower, Dwight	1953–61
Fillmore, Millard	1850–53	Kennedy, John F.	1961–63
Pierce, Franklin	1853–57	Johnson, Lyndon	1963–69
Buchanan, James	1857–61	Nixon, Richard	1969–74
Lincoln, Abraham	1861–65	Ford, Gerald	1974–77
Johnson, Andrew	1865–69	Carter, Jimmy	1977–81
Grant, Ulysses S.	1869–77	Reagan, Ronald	1981–89
Hayes, Rutherford B.	1877–81	Bush, George H.W.	1989–93
Garfield, James	1881	Clinton, William J.	1993–2001
Arthur, Chester	1881–85	Bush, George W.	2001–09
Cleveland, Grover	1885–89	Obama, Barack	2009–17
		Trump, Donald	2017-present

B. The Bill of Rights

Amendment I

Congress shall make no law respecting an establishment of religion, or prohibiting the free exercise thereof; or abridging the freedom of speech, or of the press; or the right of the people peaceably to assemble, and to petition the government for a redress of grievances.

Amendment II

A well regulated militia, being necessary to the security of a free state, the right of the people to keep and bear arms, shall not be infringed.

Amendment III

No soldier shall, in time of peace be quartered in any house, without the consent of the owner, nor in time of war, but in a manner to be prescribed by law.

Amendment IV

The right of the people to be secure in their persons, houses, papers, and effects, against unreasonable searches and seizures, shall not be violated, and no warrants shall issue, but upon probable cause, supported by oath or affirmation, and particularly describing the place to be searched, and the persons or things to be seized.

Amendment V

No person shall be held to answer for a capital, or otherwise infamous crime, unless on a presentment or indictment of a grand jury, except in cases arising in the land or naval forces, or in the militia, when in actual service in time of war or public danger; nor shall any person be subject for the same offense to be twice put in jeopardy of life or limb; nor shall be compelled in any criminal case to be a witness against himself, nor be deprived of life, liberty, or property, without due process of law; nor shall private property be taken for public use, without just compensation.

Amendment VI

In all criminal prosecutions, the accused shall enjoy the right to a speedy and public trial, by an impartial jury of the state and district wherein the crime shall have been committed, which district shall have been previously ascertained by law, and to be informed of the nature and cause of the accusation; to be confronted with the witnesses against him; to have compulsory process for obtaining witnesses in his favor, and to have the assistance of counsel for his defense.

Amendment VII

In suits at common law, where the value in controversy shall exceed twenty dollars, the right of trial by jury shall be preserved, and no fact tried by a jury, shall be otherwise reexamined in any court of the United States, than according to the rules of the common law.

Amendment VIII

Excessive bail shall not be required, nor excessive fines imposed, nor cruel and unusual punishments inflicted.

Amendment IX

The enumeration in the Constitution, of certain rights, shall not be construed to deny or disparage others retained by the people.

Amendment X

The powers not delegated to the United States by the Constitution, nor prohibited by it to the states, are reserved to the states respectively, or to the people.

C. The Declaration of Independence

IN CONGRESS, July 4, 1776.

The unanimous Declaration of the thirteen united States of America,

When in the Course of human events, it becomes necessary for one people to dissolve the political bands which have connected them with another, and to assume among the powers of the earth, the separate and equal station to which the Laws of Nature and of Nature's God entitle them, a decent respect to the opinions of mankind requires that they should declare the causes which impel them to the separation.

We hold these truths to be self-evident, that all men are created equal, that they are endowed by their Creator with certain unalienable Rights, that among these are Life, Liberty and the pursuit of Happiness.—That to secure these rights, Governments are instituted among Men, deriving their just powers from the consent of the governed,—That whenever any Form of Government becomes destructive of these ends, it is the Right of the People to alter or to abolish it, and to institute new Government, laying its foundation on such principles and organizing its powers in such form, as to them shall seem most likely to effect their Safety and Happiness. Prudence, indeed, will dictate that Governments long established should not be changed for light and transient causes; and accordingly all experience hath shewn, that mankind are more disposed to suffer, while evils are sufferable, than to right themselves by abolishing the forms to which they are accustomed. But when a long train of abuses and usurpations, pursuing invariably the same Object evinces a design to reduce them under absolute Despotism, it is their right, it is their duty, to throw off such Government, and to provide new Guards for their future security.—Such has been the patient sufferance of these Colonies; and such is now the necessity which constrains them to alter their former Systems of Government. The history of the present King of Great Britain is a history of repeated injuries and usurpations, all having in direct object the establishment of an absolute Tyranny over these States. To prove this, let Facts be submitted to a candid world.

He has refused his Assent to Laws, the most wholesome and necessary for the public good.

He has forbidden his Governors to pass Laws of immediate and pressing importance, unless suspended in their operation till his Assent should be obtained; and when so suspended, he has utterly neglected to attend to them.

He has refused to pass other Laws for the accommodation of large districts of people, unless those people would relinquish the right of Representation in the Legislature, a right inestimable to them and formidable to tyrants only.

He has called together legislative bodies at places unusual, uncomfortable, and distant from the depository of their public Records, for the sole purpose of fatiguing them into compliance with his measures.

He has dissolved Representative Houses repeatedly, for opposing with manly firmness his invasions on the rights of the people.

He has refused for a long time, after such dissolutions, to cause others to be elected; whereby the Legislative powers, incapable of Annihilation, have returned to the People at large for their exercise; the State remaining in the mean time exposed to all the dangers of invasion from without, and convulsions within.

He has endeavoured to prevent the population of these States; for that purpose obstructing the Laws for Naturalization of Foreigners; refusing to pass others to encourage their migrations hither, and raising the conditions of new Appropriations of Lands.

He has obstructed the Administration of Justice, by refusing his Assent to Laws for establishing Judiciary powers.

He has made Judges dependent on his Will alone, for the tenure of their offices, and the amount and payment of their salaries.

He has erected a multitude of New Offices, and sent hither swarms of Officers to harrass our people, and eat out their substance.

He has kept among us, in times of peace, Standing Armies without the Consent of our legislatures.

He has affected to render the Military independent of and superior to the Civil power.

He has combined with others to subject us to a jurisdiction foreign to our constitution, and unacknowledged by our laws; giving his Assent to their Acts of pretended Legislation:

For Quartering large bodies of armed troops among us:

For protecting them, by a mock Trial, from punishment for any Murders which they should commit on the Inhabitants of these States:

For cutting off our Trade with all parts of the world:

For imposing Taxes on us without our Consent:

For depriving us in many cases, of the benefits of Trial by Jury:

For transporting us beyond Seas to be tried for pretended offences

For abolishing the free System of English Laws in a neighbouring Province, establishing therein an Arbitrary government, and enlarging its Boundaries so as to render it at once an example and fit instrument for introducing the same absolute rule into these Colonies:

For taking away our Charters, abolishing our most valuable Laws, and altering fundamentally the Forms of our Governments:

For suspending our own Legislatures, and declaring themselves invested with power to legislate for us in all cases whatsoever.

He has abdicated Government here, by declaring us out of his Protection and waging War against us.

He has plundered our seas, ravaged our Coasts, burnt our towns, and destroyed the lives of our people.

He is at this time transporting large Armies of foreign Mercenaries to compleat the works of death, desolation and tyranny, already begun with circumstances of Cruelty & perfidy scarcely paralleled in the most barbarous ages, and totally unworthy the Head of a civilized nation.

He has constrained our fellow Citizens taken Captive on the high Seas to bear Arms against their Country, to become the executioners of their friends and Brethren, or to fall themselves by their Hands.

He has excited domestic insurrections amongst us, and has endeavoured to bring on the inhabitants of our frontiers, the merciless Indian Savages, whose known rule of warfare, is an undistinguished destruction of all ages, sexes and conditions.

In every stage of these Oppressions We have Petitioned for Redress in the most humble terms: Our repeated Petitions have been answered only by repeated injury. A Prince whose character is thus marked by every act which may define a Tyrant, is unfit to be the ruler of a free people.

Nor have We been wanting in attentions to our Brittish brethren. We have warned them from time to time of attempts by their legislature to extend an unwarrantable jurisdiction over us. We have reminded them of the circumstances of our emigration and settlement here. We have appealed to their native justice and magnanimity, and we have conjured them by the ties of our common kindred to disavow these usurpations, which, would inevitably interrupt our connections and correspondence. They too have been deaf to the voice of justice and of consanguinity. We must, therefore, acquiesce in the necessity, which denounces our Separation, and hold them, as we hold the rest of mankind, Enemies in War, in Peace Friends.

We, therefore, the Representatives of the united States of America, in General Congress, Assembled, appealing to the Supreme Judge of the world for the rectitude of our intentions, do, in the Name, and by Authority of the good People of these Colonies, solemnly publish and declare, That these United Colonies are, and of Right ought to be Free and Independent States; that they are Absolved from all Allegiance to the British Crown, and that all political connection between them and the State of Great Britain, is and ought to be totally dissolved; and that as Free and Independent States, they have full Power to levy War, conclude Peace, contract Alliances, establish Commerce, and to do all other Acts and Things which Independent States may of right do. And for the support of this Declaration, with a firm reliance on the protection of divine Providence, we mutually pledge to each other our Lives, our Fortunes and our sacred Honor.

The 56 signatures on the Declaration appear in the positions indicated:

Column 1

Georgia:

Button Gwinnett

Lyman Hall

George Walton

Column 2

North Carolina:

William Hooper

Joseph Hewes

John Penn

South Carolina:

Edward Rutledge

Thomas Heyward, Jr.

Thomas Lynch, Jr.

Arthur Middleton

Column 3

Massachusetts:

John Hancock

Maryland:

Samuel Chase

William Paca

Thomas Stone

Charles Carroll of Carrollton

Virginia:

George Wythe

Richard Henry Lee

Thomas Jefferson

Benjamin Harrison

Thomas Nelson, Jr.

Francis Lightfoot Lee

Carter Braxton

Column 4

Pennsylvania:

Robert Morris

Benjamin Rush

Benjamin Franklin

John Morton

George Clymer

James Smith

George Taylor

James Wilson

George Ross

Delaware:

Caesar Rodney

George Read

Thomas McKean

Column 5

New York:

William Floyd

Philip Livingston

Francis Lewis

Lewis Morris

New Jersey:

Richard Stockton

John Witherspoon

Francis Hopkinson

John Hart

Abraham Clark

Column 6

New Hampshire:

Josiah Bartlett

William Whipple

Massachusetts:

Samuel Adams

John Adams

Robert Treat Paine

Elbridge Gerry

Rhode Island:

Stephen Hopkins

William Ellery

Connecticut:

Roger Sherman

Samuel Huntington

William Williams

Oliver Wolcott

New Hampshire:

Matthew Thornton

GLOSSARY

abolish (uh-BOL-ish) to do away with, bring to an end

abolitionists (a-buh-LI-shun-ists) people who wanted to end slavery in the United States

accomplishments (uh-COM-plish-munts) achievements; positive things that are done

agrarian (uh-GRAR-ee-un) having to do with the land and farming interests

agricultural (ag-ri-KUL-chur-ul) having to do with farming

Alamo (A-luh-moh) an old mission in San Antonio, Texas, where the Mexican army defeated the Texan army in a battle for Texas independence

alliance (uh-LY-unts) an agreement among nations

Allies (A-lyz) in World War I, France, Great Britain, Russia, and (later) Italy and the United States; in World War II, the United States, Great Britain, the Soviet Union, and others.

amendments (uh-MEND-munts) changes to the U.S. Constitution

American Federation of Labor (AFL) (uh-MER-uh-kun fe-duh-RAY-shun UV LAY-bur) the largest workers' union in America, founded in 1890

amphibious (am-FI-bee-us) able to operate on sea or land

annex (a-NEKS) to add a piece of land to a larger territory

appointed (uh-POYN-tid) chosen for an official position or task

---

PRONUNCIATION KEY

CAPITAL LETTERS show the stressed syllables.

a	as in m**a**t	f	as in **f**it
ay	as in d**ay**, s**ay**	g	as in **g**o
ch	as in **ch**ew	i	as in s**i**t
e	as in b**e**d	j	as in **j**ob, **g**em
ee	as in **e**ven, **ea**sy, n**ee**d	k	as in **c**ool, **k**ey

arbitration (ar-buh-TRAY-shun) when two sides agree to follow the ruling of a third party who has no loyalties to either side

Articles of Confederation (AR-ti-kulz UV kun-fe-duh-RAY-shun) guidelines for the new government of the United States, written in 1775

authority (uh-THOR-uh-tee) power; the right to command others

authorized (AW-thur-eyezd) officially allowed; given permission by a person in power

baby boom (BAY-bee BOOM) the population explosion that took place in the United States after World War II

Battle of the Coral Sea (BA-tul UV THUH KOR-ul SEE) May 1942 battle off Australia that was a turning point in World War II

bicameral (by-KAM-uh-rul) having two houses, or parts, as in a legislature

Bill of Rights (BIL UV RYTS) the first ten amendments to the Constitution; defines the basic rights of all people living in the United States

black codes (BLAK KOHDZ) laws passed by southern states to limit the rights of African Americans

Black Tuesday (BLAK TOOZ-day) October 29, 1929, the day the U.S. stock market crashed

blockade (blo-KAYD) the use of warships to block merchant vessels

Boston Massacre (BOS-tun MA-si-kur) an event in 1770 in which English soldiers shot at a crowd in Boston and killed several people

---

PRONUNCIATION KEY

CAPITAL LETTERS show the stressed syllables.

a	as in m**a**t	f	as in **f**it
ay	as in d**ay**, s**ay**	g	as in **g**o
ch	as in **ch**ew	i	as in s**i**t
e	as in b**e**d	j	as in **j**ob, **g**em
ee	as in **e**ven, **ea**sy, n**ee**d	k	as in **c**ool, **k**ey

Boston Tea Party (BOS-tun TEE PAR-tee) an event in 1773 in which colonists protested by throwing tea into Boston Harbor

boycott (BOY-kot) a protest in which people refuse to buy the products or use the services of a certain business

Cabinet (KAB-uh-nit) a group of people who advise the president

California Gold Rush (ka-luh-FOR-nyuh GOLD RUSH) the migration, or movement, of people to California in 1849 to look for gold

Canal Era (kuh-NAL AR-uh) period between 1825 and 1840 when many canals, or inland waterways, were built in the United States

capitalist economy (KA-pi-tul-ist i-KO-nuh-mee) a system in which people can own their own businesses and land

CCC (SEE-SEE-SEE) the Civilian Conservation Corps, created in 1933 to provide jobs for young men between 18 and 25

Central Powers (SEN-trul POW-urz) in World War I, Germany, Austria-Hungary, and Italy (until 1915)

checks and balances (CHEKS AND BA-lun-ses) a system that allows each branch of government to check, or control, the other two branches

child labor (CHILD LAY-bur) the employment of children, often in poor conditions

Chinese Exclusion Act (chy-nees ecks-KLOO-zhun AKT) law passed by Congress in 1882 that ended immigration into the United States for all Chinese people

---

PRONUNCIATION KEY

CAPITAL LETTERS show the stressed syllables.

ng	as in runni**ng**	u	as in b**u**t, s**o**me
o	as in c**o**t, f**a**ther	uh	as in **a**bout, tak**e**n, lem**o**n, penc**i**l
oh	as in g**o**, n**o**te	ur	as in t**er**m
sh	as in **sh**y	y	as in l**i**ne, fl**y**
th	as in **th**in	zh	as in vi**s**ion, mea**s**ure
oo	as in t**oo**		

Civil Rights Act of 1957 (SI-vul RYTS AKT UV nyn-TEEN FIF-tee SE-vun) an act designed to make sure that African Americans could use their right to vote

Civil War (SI-vul WAUR) the period in U.S. history from 1861 to 1865, when the North and South fought as two separate nations

Cold War (KOHLD WAUR) a period of competition between the Soviet Union and the United States for power and influence in the world

collective bargaining (kuh-LEK-tiv BAR-gun-ing) discussions between a labor union and management

colonies (KO-luh-nees) regions controlled by distant countries

colonists (KO-luh-nists) people who move to another country but who are still ruled by their native country

commander in chief (kuh-MAN-dur IN CHEEF) the person in charge of the American army

commerce (KO-murs) the buying and selling of goods

Commonwealth of Independent States (KOM-un-welth UV in-duh-PEN-dunt STAYTS) the union of free, independent countries formed in the late 1980s and 1990s from former Soviet Union satellite nations

communist (KOM-yuh-nist) relating to communism; a political system in which all property and businesses belong to the government

commuter (kuh-MYOOT-ur) someone who commutes, or travels from home to work, regularly

---

PRONUNCIATION KEY

CAPITAL LETTERS show the stressed syllables.

a	as in m**a**t	f	as in **f**it
ay	as in d**ay**, s**ay**	g	as in **g**o
ch	as in **ch**ew	i	as in s**i**t
e	as in b**e**d	j	as in **j**ob, **g**em
ee	as in **e**ven, **ea**sy, n**ee**d	k	as in **c**ool, **k**ey

compromise (KOM-pruh-myz) an agreement in which both sides give up a little and receive a little

concurrent powers (kun-KUR-unt POW-urz) powers shared by the national and state governments

Confederate States of America (kun-FE-duh-rit STAYTS UV uh-MER-i-kuh) the separate nation formed by the southern states after they seceded from the United States in 1861

confederation (kun-fe-duh-RAY-shun) a group of states or nations that band together for a purpose but still remain independent

congress (KON-gris) a group of people who represent, or stand for, other people

Congress (KON-gris) the law-making branch of the government; also called the *legislature*

conservatives (kun-SUR-vuh-tivs) people who do not believe in government action to solve social problems

Constitution (kon-sti-TOO-shun) the document written in Philadelphia in 1787 that replaced the Articles of Confederation; the highest law in the land

Constitutional Convention (kon-sti-TOO-shun-ul kun-VEN-shun) the meeting held in Philadelphia in 1787 during which state delegates wrote the Constitution

consumer goods (kun-SOO-mur GOODS) items such as cars, furniture, and clothes

---

PRONUNCIATION KEY

CAPITAL LETTERS show the stressed syllables.

ng	as in runni**ng**	u	as in b**u**t, s**o**me
o	as in c**o**t, f**a**ther	uh	as in **a**bout, tak**e**n, lem**o**n, penc**il**
oh	as in g**o**, n**o**te	ur	as in t**er**m
sh	as in **sh**y	y	as in l**i**ne, fl**y**
th	as in **th**in	zh	as in vi**s**ion, mea**s**ure
oo	as in t**oo**		

conveyor belt (kun-VAY-ur BELT) a belt that moves materials and products from one part of a factory to another

corporations (kor-pur-AY-shuns) large businesses that are owned by many stockholders

D-Day (DEE DAY) June 6, 1944, the day Allied troops landed at Normandy, France to fight the German army

debt (DET) money owed to someone else

Declaration of Independence (de-kluh-RAY-shun UV IN-duh-PEN-dens) the document that declared the colonists' independence from England, written in 1776

delegates (DEL-uh-guts) people who are chosen to attend a convention (meeting) on behalf of others

democracy (di-MO-kruh-see) a form of government that is run by the people it serves

Democratic-Republican Party (de-muh-KRA-tik ri-PUB-li-kin PAR-tee) a political party that followed the ideas of Thomas Jefferson

dictator (DIK-tay-tur) someone who takes complete control of a government

dollar diplomacy (DO-lur di-PLOH-muh-see) the investment of American money overseas not only in order to help other nations, but also to gain power for the United States

draft (DRAFT) mandatory service in the armed forces

PRONUNCIATION KEY

CAPITAL LETTERS show the stressed syllables.

a	as in m**a**t	f	as in **f**it
ay	as in d**ay**, s**ay**	g	as in **g**o
ch	as in **ch**ew	i	as in s**i**t
e	as in b**e**d	j	as in **j**ob, **g**em
ee	as in **e**ven, **ea**sy, n**ee**d	k	as in **c**ool, **k**ey

economy (ee-KON-uh-mee) a nation's sources of wealth and how they are managed

Elastic Clause (i-LAS-tik KLAWZ) another name for the Necessary and Proper Clause

Emancipation Proclamation (i-man-suh-PAY-shun pro-kluh-MAY-shun) a declaration that freed all slaves in the South, issued by President Abraham Lincoln in 1863

emigrated (EM-uh-gray-tud) left their homeland to live elsewhere

ethnic group (ETH-nik GROOP) people who share a similar culture and country of origin

executive branch (eg-ZEK-yuh-tiv BRANCH) the part of government responsible for enforcing, or carrying out, laws

expressed powers (ek-SPRESD POW-urz) powers that the Constitution specifically gives to the federal government

factory towns (FAK-tuh-ree TOWNZ) towns where most people either worked for the factory or depended on it

Fair Labor Standards Act (FAYR LAY-bur STAN-durdz AKT) 1937 law to set a minimum wage

famine (FA-min) a shortage of food

federal (FE-uh-rul) national; having to do with the central government rather than the individual states

Federal Trade Commission (FTC) (FE-duh-rul TRAYD kuh-MI-shun) a government department that works to prevent unfair trade practices

---

PRONUNCIATION KEY

CAPITAL LETTERS show the stressed syllables.

ng as in runni**ng**

o as in c**o**t, f**a**ther

oh as in g**o**, n**o**te

sh as in **sh**y

th as in **th**in

oo as in t**oo**

u as in b**u**t, s**o**me

uh as in **a**bout, tak**e**n, lem**o**n, penc**il**

ur as in t**er**m

y as in l**i**ne, fl**y**

zh as in vi**s**ion, mea**s**ure

federalism (FED-ur-ul-iz-um) the division of power between the national, or federal, government and state governments

Federalist Party (FED-ur-ul-ist PAR-tee) a political party that followed the ideas of Alexander Hamilton

Fifteenth Amendment (fif-TEENTH uh-MEND-munt) an amendment to the Constitution passed in 1870; declares that the right to vote cannot be denied on account of race, color, or previous condition of servitude (slavery)

foreign policy (FOR-in PO-luh-see) the political dealings of one country with other countries around the world

foreigners (FOR-i-nurz) people from other countries who live in a host country

Forty-niners (FOR-tee-NY-nurz) people who traveled to California in 1849 to search for gold

Founding Fathers (FOWND-ing FO-thurz) the men who were part of the first federal government set up under the U.S. Constitution

Fourteenth Amendment (fohr-TEENTH uh-MEND-munt) an amendment to the Constitution passed in 1868; guarantees civil rights to all citizens

free state (FREE STAYT) a state that did not allow slavery

Freedmen's Bureau (FREED-menz BYUR-oh) a government organization that helped former slaves get food, housing, and education after the Civil War

---

PRONUNCIATION KEY

CAPITAL LETTERS show the stressed syllables.

a	as in m**a**t	f	as in **f**it
ay	as in d**ay**, s**ay**	g	as in **g**o
ch	as in **ch**ew	i	as in s**i**t
e	as in b**e**d	j	as in **j**ob, **g**em
ee	as in **e**ven, **ea**sy, n**ee**d	k	as in **c**ool, **k**ey

frontier (frun-TEER) the boundary between settled and unsettled territories

Gadsden Purchase (GADZ-den PUR-chus) an action in which the United States bought southern Arizona and the rest of New Mexico from Mexico for $10 million

geography (jee-O-gruh-fee) the location and physical features of an area

Gettysburg Address (GE-teez-burg uh-DRES) Abraham Lincoln's 1863 speech at the cemetery in Gettysburg, Pennsylvania, after the Battle of Gettysburg

GI Bill (JEE-EYE BIL) 1944 law that gave World War II veterans unemployment insurance, loans for building homes and starting businesses, medical treatment, vocational training, and education

Great Depression (GRAYT de-PRESH-un) period from 1929 through the 1930s when the United States, and much of the world, suffered from a major economic slowdown

governor (GUV-ur-nur) the person in charge of running a colony or a state

guarantee (gar-un-TEE) an official promise

Holocaust (HOL-uh-kost) the mass slaughter of Jews and others by Germany during World War II

Homestead Act (HOHM-sted AKT) an 1862 law that gave a 160-acre plot on the western plains to anyone willing to farm the land

homesteader (HOHM-ste-dur) a person willing to take over land in the frontier area and build a home on it

---

PRONUNCIATION KEY

CAPITAL LETTERS show the stressed syllables.

ng as in runni**ng**

o as in c**o**t, f**a**ther

oh as in g**o**, n**o**te

sh as in **sh**y

th as in **th**in

oo as in t**oo**

u as in b**u**t, s**o**me

uh as in **a**bout, tak**e**n, lem**o**n, penc**il**

ur as in t**er**m

y as in l**i**ne, fl**y**

zh as in vi**s**ion, mea**s**ure

House of Representatives (HOWS UV rep-ri-ZEN-tuh-tivz) one of the houses of Congress; membership depends on the population of each state

immigrants (I-mi-grunts) people who move to a country that is not their native land

impeach (im-PEECH) to accuse an elected official of wrongdoing and to hold a special trial

imperialism (im-PIR-ee-uh-liz-um) building an empire by taking land in other parts of the world

implied powers (im-PLYD POW-urz) powers that are given to the federal government, but are not directly stated in the Constitution

Indian Wars (IN-dee-un WAURZ) battles fought between American settlers and Native Americans over western territories

Indians (IN-dee-uns) native peoples of North America to whom European explorers gave this name in the mistaken belief that they had arrived in India

industrial (in-DUS-tree-ul) based on factory production

Industrial Revolution (in-DUS-tree-ul re-vuh-LOO-shun) major changes brought about by the invention of machines that could do the work of many people

interchangeable parts (in-tur-CHAYN-juh-bul PARTS) parts made the same way each time so that they always fit with other parts

internationalism (in-tur-NA-shuh-nuh-liz-um) a policy of establishing relations with other nations

---

PRONUNCIATION KEY

CAPITAL LETTERS show the stressed syllables.

a	as in m**a**t	f	as in **f**it
ay	as in d**ay**, s**ay**	g	as in **g**o
ch	as in **ch**ew	i	as in s**i**t
e	as in b**e**d	j	as in **j**ob, **g**em
ee	as in **e**ven, **ea**sy, n**ee**d	k	as in **c**ool, **k**ey

interpreted (in-TUR-pruh-tud) understood and explained to others

invasion (in-VAY-zhun) an attack into another nation's territory

investors (in-VEST-urs) people who put money into, or invest in, businesses

Iron Curtain (EYE-urn KUR-tun) the imaginary line between the West and the Soviet Union and its satellite countries

isolationist (eye-suh-LAY-shun-ist) avoiding political and economic involvement with other countries

issue currency (I-shoo KUR-in-see) make paper money and coins

Jazz Age (JAZ AYJ) period after World War I when entertainment such as jazz music and dancing became popular

judicial branch (joo-DI-shul BRANCH) the part of the government responsible for interpreting laws

Know-Nothing Party (NOH-NUH-thing PAR-tee) a political party based on prejudice against foreigners, formed in the 1860s and soon abandoned

Ku Klux Klan (KOO KLUCKS KLAN) a secret organization formed by white southerners who used terror to scare African Americans and gain white control

League of Nations (LEEG UV NAY-shuns) an international organization formed after World War I to keep peace in the world

legislative branch (LE-jis-lay-tiv BRANCH) the part of the government responsible for making laws

---

PRONUNCIATION KEY

CAPITAL LETTERS show the stressed syllables.

ng as in runni**ng**

o as in c**o**t, f**a**ther

oh as in g**o**, n**o**te

sh as in **sh**y

th as in **th**in

oo as in t**oo**

u as in b**u**t, s**o**me

uh as in **a**bout, tak**e**n, lem**o**n, penc**il**

ur as in t**er**m

y as in l**i**ne, fl**y**

zh as in vi**s**ion, mea**s**ure

legislature (LE-jis-lay-chur) the law-making branch of the state or federal government

liberals (LI-bur-uls) people who believe in government action to solve social problems

limited war (LIM-uh-tid WAUR) a war in which the goal is not complete victory over another nation, but some more narrow aim

Lone Star Republic (LOHN STAR ri-PUH-blik) the name given to Texas after it declared its independence from Mexico in 1836

loom (LOOM) a machine that weaves thread into cloth

Louisiana Purchase (loo-ee-zee-A-nuh PUR-chus) an action in which the United States bought a huge area of land around the Mississippi River and farther west; it was purchased from France for $15 million

Loyalists (LOY-uh-lists) colonists who remained loyal to England during the American Revolution

majority (muh-JOR-uh-tee) more than half of any group

Manifest Destiny (MAN-uh-fest DES-ti-nee) the belief of many Americans that westward expansion was a right given to them by God

Marshall Plan (MAR-shul PLAN) the 1947 plan for sending billions of U.S. dollars to help European countries recover from World War II

mass production (MAS pruh-DUK-shun) the making of things in large amounts and for less money

merchant vessels (MURCH-unt VES-uls) ships that carry goods from one place to another; trading ships

PRONUNCIATION KEY

CAPITAL LETTERS show the stressed syllables.

a	as in m**a**t	f	as in **f**it
ay	as in d**ay**, s**ay**	g	as in **g**o
ch	as in **ch**ew	i	as in s**i**t
e	as in b**e**d	j	as in **j**ob, **g**em
ee	as in **e**ven, **ea**sy, n**ee**d	k	as in **c**ool, **k**ey

Mexican Cession (MEK-si-kun SE-shun) the territory Mexico sold to the United States in 1848, including Texas, California, and much of New Mexico

middle class (MID-ul KLAS) people who are neither upper class nor lower class; includes business people, farmers, professionals, and skilled workers

migration (my-GRAY-shun) large movement of people or animals

mill (MIL) factory

Missouri Compromise (miz-OOR-ee KOM-pruh-myz) the 1820 agreement that let Maine join the United States as a free state and Missouri join as a slave state

Monroe Doctrine (mun-ROH DOK-trin) an 1823 policy stating that the United States would no longer interfere in European affairs, and that Europe could no longer interfere in the affairs of the Americas

National Aeronautics and Space Administration (NASA) (NA-suh) the agency responsible for manned and unmanned space flights

nationalism (NA-shuh-nul-iz-um) a feeling of pride in one's country

Native Americans (NAY-tiv uh-MER-i-kunz) people who lived in North America before the Europeans arrived; also called *Indians*

naturalization (na-chuh-rul-eye-ZAY-shun) the process by which a foreign-born person becomes a citizen of the United States

Necessary and Proper Clause (NE-suh-ser-ee AND PRO-pur KLAUZ) a section of the Constitution that gives the national government the power to make all laws necessary to carry out expressed powers

---

PRONUNCIATION KEY

CAPITAL LETTERS show the stressed syllables.

ng as in runni**ng**

o as in c**o**t, f**a**ther

oh as in g**o**, n**o**te

sh as in **sh**y

th as in **th**in

oo as in t**oo**

u as in b**u**t, s**o**me

uh as in **a**bout, tak**e**n, lem**o**n, penc**i**l

ur as in t**er**m

y as in l**i**ne, fl**y**

zh as in vi**s**ion, mea**s**ure

neutral (NOO-trul) taking no official side in political disagreements

neutrality (noo-TRAL-i-tee) a policy of not taking sides in political disagreements

New Deal (NOO DEEL) President Roosevelt's 1930s plan to help the U.S. economy

New World (NOO WURLD) the name European explorers gave to North America

nomadic (noh-MA-dik) moving from place to place

North Atlantic Treaty Organization (NATO) (NAY-toh) the protective agency founded by Western nations in 1949 as protection against the Soviet Union

Northwest Territory (north-WEST TER-i-tor-ee) land northwest of the original 13 states that became American territory as part of the 1783 Treaty of Paris

nullify (NUHL-i-fy) to say that a law has no force or power

oath (OHTH) a solemn, official promise

omnibus (OM-ni-bus) one of the first forms of public transportation; a horse-drawn streetcar from which the word *bus* derives

open immigration policy (OH-pun im-i-GRAY-shun POL-uh-see) a situation in which a nation sets no limits on how many people can enter, or immigrate to, the country each year

Oregon Country (OR-i-gon KUN-tree) the northwestern part of the United States, added to the nation's territory in the late 1840s

PRONUNCIATION KEY

CAPITAL LETTERS show the stressed syllables.

a	as in m**a**t	f	as in **f**it
ay	as in d**ay**, s**ay**	g	as in **g**o
ch	as in **ch**ew	i	as in s**i**t
e	as in b**e**d	j	as in **j**ob, **g**em
ee	as in **e**ven, **ea**sy, n**ee**d	k	as in **c**ool, **k**ey

originate (or-I-ji-nayt) to start in; to come from

Parliament (PARL-uh-munt) the British legislature

pension (PEN-shun) a payment to someone who has retired because of age

philosophy (fi-LO-suh-fee) a way of thinking

plantations (plan-TAY-shuns) large farms in the southern United States; most used slave labor until the end of the Civil War

platform (PLAT-form) a political party's statement of its main goals

political party (puh-LI-ti-kul PAR-tee) a group of people who share the same ideas about government

Populist Party (POP-yoo-list PAR-tee) 1890s American political party formed to give more power to farmers and laborers

prejudice (PRE-juh-dis) negative judgments or opinions people have toward others who are different from them

Progressive movement (pruh-GRES-iv MOOV-munt) a time of major reform of America's economic and political institutions, from about 1890 to 1917

prohibited (proh-HIB-i-tud) forbade; outlawed

Prohibition (proh-uh-BI-shun) the period during which alcohol was banned in the United States; it was brought about by the Eighteenth Amendment in 1919 and repealed by the Twenty-First Amendment in 1933

PRONUNCIATION KEY

CAPITAL LETTERS show the stressed syllables.

ng	as in runni**ng**	u	as in b**u**t, s**o**me
o	as in c**o**t, f**a**ther	uh	as in **a**bout, tak**e**n, lem**o**n, penc**i**l
oh	as in g**o**, n**o**te	ur	as in t**er**m
sh	as in **sh**y	y	as in l**i**ne, fl**y**
th	as in **th**in	zh	as in vi**s**ion, mea**s**ure
oo	as in t**oo**		

propaganda (pro-puh-GAN-duh) spreading ideas in order to convince people to feel or think a certain way

prospector (PRO-spek-tur) a person looking for mineral riches, as during the California Gold Rush

prosperity (pro-SPER-i-tee) a time when the economy is doing well and people have enough money and goods

public works projects (PUB-lik WURKS PRO-jekts) construction and repair projects paid for by the government

quotas (KWOH-tuz) limits on the number of immigrants allowed into the United States each year

racial discrimination (RAY-shul dis-krim-i-NAY-shun) unfairness to someone based on race, as in hiring for a job

Radicals (RA-di-kulz) a group of Republicans in Congress who helped pass Constitutional amendments protecting the rights of African Americans

ratified (RA-ti-fyd) accepted by the states through a vote

raw materials (RAUW muh-TIR-ee-ulz) materials or goods needed to make a final product

reconcile (REH-kun-syl) to work out one's problems with someone else

Reconstruction (ree-kun-STRUK-shun) the period after the Civil War when the South was rebuilt

Redcoats (RED-kohts) nickname for English soldiers during the American Revolution

---

PRONUNCIATION KEY

CAPITAL LETTERS show the stressed syllables.

a	as in m**a**t	f	as in **f**it
ay	as in d**ay**, s**ay**	g	as in **g**o
ch	as in **ch**ew	i	as in s**i**t
e	as in b**e**d	j	as in **j**ob, **g**em
ee	as in **e**ven, **ea**sy, n**ee**d	k	as in **c**ool, **k**ey

reform movements (ri-FORM MOOV-munts) efforts by groups of people who want to change social conditions for the better

religious freedom (ruh-LI-jus FREE-dum) the right to follow one's religious beliefs

representatives (rep-ri-ZEN-tuh-tivz) members of the House of Representatives; people who are elected to speak for many others and work for their benefit

Republican Party (ruh-PUB-li-kin PAR-tee) a political party formed in 1854 that focused on ending slavery in the new territories of the United States

reservation (rez-ur-VAY-shun) land that is set aside, or reserved, for a special purpose

reserved powers (ri-ZURVD POW-urz) powers that are reserved, or set aside, for the state governments

restrictions (reh-STRIK-shuns) limits

revise (ree-VYZ) to change or rework

revolution (rev-uh-LOO-shun) a fight to overthrow a government

Roaring Twenties (ROR-ing TWEN-teez) the 1920s in the United States, when many inventions and new technology made life easier and helped create new jobs

sanitation (san-uh-TAY-shun) a system for keeping a community clean and healthy

secede (suh-SEED) to leave, or withdraw from, an association or a group

PRONUNCIATION KEY

CAPITAL LETTERS show the stressed syllables.

ng as in runni**ng**

o as in c**o**t, f**a**ther

oh as in g**o**, n**o**te

sh as in **sh**y

th as in **th**in

oo as in t**oo**

u as in b**u**t, s**o**me

uh as in **a**bout, tak**e**n, lem**o**n, penc**i**l

ur as in t**er**m

y as in l**i**ne, fl**y**

zh as in vi**s**ion, mea**s**ure

Second Continental Congress (SE-kund kon-tin-EN-tul KON-gris) the group of state delegates who set up the colonial army, wrote the Declaration of Independence, and wrote the Articles of Confederation

secretary of state (SE-kruh-ter-ee UV STAYT) the person responsible for the foreign policy of the United States

secretary of the treasury (SE-kruh-ter-ee UV THUH TRE-zhuh-ree) the person responsible for collecting, managing, and spending government money

security (suh-KYUR-i-tee) safety

Selective Service Act (suh-LEK-tiv SUR-vis AKT) 1940 law that set up the first peacetime draft

self-government (SELF-GUV-urn-mint) government controlled by the people it serves

Senate (SE-nut) one of the houses of Congress; each state is represented by two senators

senators (SEN-uh-turz) members of the Senate

separation of powers (se-puh-RAY-shun UV POW-urz) the division of the U.S. government into three branches

servitude (SUR-vuh-tood) slavery

Seward's Folly (SOO-wurdz FO-lee) the name Americans gave to Secretary of State William Seward's purchase of Alaska in 1867

PRONUNCIATION KEY

CAPITAL LETTERS show the stressed syllables.

a	as in m**a**t	f	as in **f**it
ay	as in d**ay**, s**ay**	g	as in **g**o
ch	as in **ch**ew	i	as in s**i**t
e	as in b**e**d	j	as in **j**ob, **g**em
ee	as in **e**ven, **ea**sy, n**ee**d	k	as in **c**ool, **k**ey

Sherman Antitrust Act (SHUR-min an-tee-TRUST AKT) a law passed in 1890 to make trusts (groups of companies that work together to squeeze their competition) illegal

siege (SEEJ) the surrounding of an area by an army in the hope that the other side will surrender

Social Security Act (SOH-shul suh-KYUR-i-tee AKT) 1935 law designed to help care for needy children and those who could not work because of poor health and to pay retired workers over 65 a continuing income

sovereignty (SOV-run-tee) the absolute, or highest, power of a state or other government

Soviet Union (SOH-vee-ut YEWN-yun) a communist state formed in 1922 that included Russia and the eastern European countries occupied by Russia at the end of World War II

speakeasies (SPEEK-ee-zees) illegal bars in the 1920s

Sputnik (SPUT-nik) the first manufactured satellite sent into outer space; it was launched by the Soviet Union in 1957 and started the race for space

stable (STAY-bul) strong and dependable

stalemate (STAYL-mayt) a situation in which neither side is winning

stocks (STOKS) shares of ownership in a company

strike (STRYK) a time when workers refuse to go to work until their demands are met by management

---

PRONUNCIATION KEY

CAPITAL LETTERS show the stressed syllables.

ng	as in runni**ng**	u	as in b**u**t, s**o**me
o	as in c**o**t, f**a**ther	uh	as in **a**bout, tak**e**n, lem**o**n, penc**il**
oh	as in g**o**, n**o**te	ur	as in t**er**m
sh	as in **sh**y	y	as in l**i**ne, fl**y**
th	as in **th**in	zh	as in vi**s**ion, mea**s**ure
oo	as in t**oo**		

suburbs (SUB-urbz) areas just outside a city where people tend to live in neighborhoods

superpowers (SOO-pur-pow-urz) nations with the greatest economic and military strength

suffrage (SUF-rij) the right to vote

tariffs (TAIR-ifs) taxes placed on certain items that are imported from other countries

taxation (tacks-AY-shun) a government's system for raising money by charging certain fees to its citizens

technology (tek-NOL-uh-jee) the ways in which science is used to solve practical problems and make life easier through inventions and innovations

temperance movement (TEM-per-unts MOOV-munt) organized effort to promote total abstinence (staying away) from alcoholic drinks

territory (TAIR-i-tor-ee) land

textile (TEKS-tyl) woven cloth

Thirteenth Amendment (thur-TEENTH uh-MEND-mint) a Constitutional amendment in 1865 that abolished all slavery in the United States

thirty-eighth parallel (thur-tee-AYTH PAR-uh-lel) the dividing line between North and South Korea

---

PRONUNCIATION KEY

CAPITAL LETTERS show the stressed syllables.

a	as in m**a**t	f	as in **f**it
ay	as in d**ay**, s**ay**	g	as in **g**o
ch	as in **ch**ew	i	as in s**i**t
e	as in b**e**d	j	as in **j**ob, **g**em
ee	as in **e**ven, **ea**sy, n**ee**d	k	as in **c**ool, **k**ey

Three-Fifths Compromise (THREE-FIFTHS KOM-pruh-myz) a compromise passed at the Constitutional Convention, stating that each slave would count as three fifths of a person

totalitarian (toh-ta-luh-TAIR-ee-un) a system of government in which the state has total control over citizens' lives

trade (TRAYD) the exchange of goods and services between one party, or one country, and another

treaty (TREE-tee) an agreement between or among countries

Treaty of Ghent (TREE-tee UV GENT) the agreement that ended the War of 1812 between the United States and England

Treaty of Paris (TREE-tee UV PAR-is) the agreement, signed in 1783, that ended the American Revolution

Treaty of Versailles (TREE-tee UV vair-SY) the 1919 treaty that officially ended World War I

trust (TRUST) a group of large companies that agree to work together in order to prevent competition from smaller companies

tyranny (TIR-uh-nee) complete control or rule by one person who does not consider the needs and wishes of the people

unions (YOON-yunz) organizations of workers who join together in an effort to protect their rights

United Nations (yoo-NY-tid NAY-shuns) an international organization founded in 1945 to keep peace in the world

urban centers (UR-bun SEN-turz) large cities

PRONUNCIATION KEY

CAPITAL LETTERS show the stressed syllables.

ng as in runni**ng**

o as in c**o**t, f**a**ther

oh as in g**o**, n**o**te

sh as in **sh**y

th as in **th**in

oo as in t**oo**

u as in b**u**t, s**o**me

uh as in **a**bout, tak**e**n, lem**o**n, penc**i**l

ur as in t**er**m

y as in l**i**ne, fl**y**

zh as in vi**s**ion, mea**s**ure

urban transportation (UR-bun trans-pur-TAY-shun) low-cost city transportation; includes buses, trolleys, subways, and elevated and commuter trains

urbanization (ur-bun-eye-ZAY-shun) the growth of cities and the movement of people to those cities

V-E Day (VEE-EE DAY) Victory in Europe Day, May 8, 1945, when World War II ended on the western front

V-J Day (VEE-JAY DAY) Victory in Japan Day, August 15, 1945, when World War II ended on the eastern front

Vietnam (VEE-et-nom) a country in Southeast Asia that was divided into two parts after French rule ended in 1954; after a long and unsuccessful war there in the 1960s, the United States finally removed its troops in 1973

War of 1812 (WAUR UV AY-teen-TWELV) a war between England and the United States, fought along the border between Canada and the United States

warlords (WAUR-lordz) aggressive military leaders; in Japan, military officers who seized control of the government in the 1920s

Warsaw Pact (WAUR-saw PAKT) the treaty between the Soviet Union and each of its satellite countries (Albania, Bulgaria, Czechoslovakia, East Germany, Hungary, Poland, Romania)

waves of immigration (WAYVS UV im-i-GRAY-shun) periods when large numbers of people enter a country

---

PRONUNCIATION KEY

CAPITAL LETTERS show the stressed syllables.

a as in m**a**t

ay as in d**ay**, s**ay**

ch as in **ch**ew

e as in b**e**d

ee as in **e**ven, **ea**sy, n**ee**d

f as in **f**it

g as in **g**o

i as in s**i**t

j as in **j**ob, **g**em

k as in **c**ool, **k**ey

westward expansion (WEST-wurd eks-PAN-shun) in U.S. history, the continued growth toward, and settlement of, the West

women's suffrage movement (WI-munz SUF-rij MOOV-munt) the organized effort to get women the right to vote

Works Progress Administration (WPA) (WERKS PROG-res ad-MIN-uh-STRAY-shun) agency created in 1935 to provide men and women with work and a chance to help society

Yankees (YANG-kees) name given to northerners by southerners

PRONUNCIATION KEY

CAPITAL LETTERS show the stressed syllables.

ng as in runni**ng**

o as in c**o**t, f**a**ther

oh as in g**o**, n**o**te

sh as in **sh**y

th as in **th**in

oo as in t**oo**

u as in b**u**t, s**o**me

uh as in **a**bout, tak**e**n, lem**o**n, penc**i**l

ur as in t**er**m

y as in l**i**ne, fl**y**

zh as in vi**s**ion, mea**s**ure

INDEX